All about
Mating, Whelping and Weaning

Puppies are terrible time-wasters – especially when you are trying to photograph them!

All about
Mating, Whelping and Weaning

DAVID CAVILL

PELHAM BOOKS

First published in Great Britain by
Pelham Books Ltd
27 Wrights Lane
London W8 5TZ
1981
Reprinted 1985, 1987

British Library Cataloguing in Publication Data

Cavill, David
    All about Mating, Whelping and Weaning.
    1. Dogs – Breeding
    I. Title
    636.7'082   SF427.2

ISBN 0 7207 1323 4

Printed and bound in Great Britain
by Butler & Tanner Ltd, Frome and London

Contents

Illustrations

Photographs

Figures

Picture credits

The photographs are by the author except the following which are reproduced courtesy of the Royal Veterinary College, University of London: pages 65, 73 and 74.
The line drawings are by Peter Willmott

For my parents (all four)

Preface

Two o'clock in the morning and Madam decides that the time has come to stop fussing and scratching about and to get on with the business of producing her first litter. She begins to strain periodically, between times looking at me with an expression combining resignation and mystification. I make a few encouraging noises – because it is my first litter too!

She heaves herself out of the whelping box, trots over to the back door and gives the short, sharp bark which means that she needs to go out. Here we are in a warm, quiet kitchen with everything ready and just waiting for her to do her bit; all she wants to do is to burrow into her hastily-dug hole in the ground beneath the holly bush. 'Bed!' I say, in my sternest voice. 'Here or nowhere!'

Kirrie gives a final push and her first whelp slides smoothly onto the mat. She looks at it in horror. She has always been the cleanest of animals and she fears that I shall be angry. She runs back to her bed, leaving the whelp and the placenta on the mat. I bend down and carefully split the membrane. As I wipe the mucus from around its mouth the whelp gurgles a little and gives a quiet cry. Kirrie is beside me suddenly, nosing into my hands. I tear the cord connecting the whelp to the placenta and put the pup into the whelping box. Kirrie jumps in and begins to lick it clean as its legs begin to beat the air. I feel quite proud!

This is a time I re-live whenever one of our bitches whelps. It is a moment which is the culmination of one of the most complex and miraculous series of actions and reactions known to Man. We are still a very long way from understanding the processes involved but we know a lot about the results of those processes. This book has been written to help both new and experienced breeders towards trouble-free whelpings – to help you feel as I do at the time of birth. It is a feeling that makes up for all the time, trouble and work that are an inevitable part of breeding dogs.

Dave Cavill 1980

Introduction

A French proverb says, 'In the beginning God made Man and, seeing him so helpless, gave him a dog.'

Throughout Man's evolution from the forests and caves of prehistory he has depended on the dog to assist him in his search for food, to guard his belongings and to control his flocks. In return Man has fed and protected his helper, and over thousands of years a unique blend of mutual affection, understanding and companionship has evolved. As Man gained greater control over his environment, he used and developed his dogs for more complex and sophisticated tasks – for fighting, guiding, pulling, pointing, retrieving and herding. The seventy-eight chromosomes of the genus canis proved to be remarkably adaptable and the range of sizes and types of dogs increased enormously as the most effective working combinations were sought, on what must have been a largely 'trial and error' basis. Throughout these ages dogs would have been whelped which were in excess of the community's needs, which were runts or just not suitable for working. Many of these would have become the first pets – playing with the children and protecting the community while the men were away. This bond of companionship and utility, built up over many thousands of years, remains to this day even though relatively few dogs are now used for working in the way they once were. As Man began to have leisure time at his disposal his dogs remained as companions but also, for many, as a means of enjoyably filling that free time. It is this factor which has led to the growth of the formalised hunting and coursing of game, the use of dogs for fighting and racing and, in the last hundred years or so, to the beauty competitions – the dog shows. These demands, coupled with the fairly constant requirement for dogs as pets and companions, gradually led to the establishment of the specialist dog breeder.

A higher proportion of British families are dog lovers and owners than in any other country in the world and, despite our quarantine restrictions, we have maintained our position as one of the foremost nations of dog breeders. One reason for this is that breeders have had a constant demand for pets which has enabled them to select the best puppies from a large number of litters, and another is the intense competition that exists within the world of dogs, whether they be for work or for show. In the same way that cars have been improved beyond recognition by the competition generated by motor racing and motor-cross and the rest, many breeds of dogs have been vastly improved in shape, size and quality compared to those bred in the past. It would also be true to say that fashion has played a part but, nevertheless, most of this gradual improvement has been instinctive and the aphorism 'mate the best to the best' still has a lot to commend it. However, much helpful research into both breeding and the

You can't help being proud of them, can you?

technical aspects of mating, whelping and weaning has been carried out during the past few years and I have tried to include as much of this information as possible.

There is one particular area of dog breeding of which we cannot be proud and this is the breeding and selling of dogs as a purely commercial venture. I do not believe that dogs are suitable animals for factory farming, whatever the demand. The man/dog relationship is one which can be best maintained by breeding in small units and this enables puppies to begin being socialised as soon as they leave the nest. Puppy farming inevitably results in puppies being deprived of human company just at the time they most need it if they are to become properly adjusted adults. To be brutally honest, there are far too many dogs being bred. The puppy farms keep up a constant supply of pups which are not only not properly domesticated but which are very often underfed and disease-prone by the time they reach a family. Added to this, the trading kennels which act as retailers for the puppy farms take no responsibility for a puppy after it has left the premises, and indeed most require the new owner to sign a form releasing the seller from his legal obligations. For these reasons puppies are often sold to unsuitable homes and good homes are often supplied with unsuitable puppies. In addition, there are the many puppies which are available as a result of the mismating of in-season pet bitches. The result is usually another dog which has to be put down or which is left on the doorstep of a rescue kennel. However, while there is a demand the unscrupulous will be prepared to meet it.

The ideal dog-owning family will take great care in selecting the breed of dog which will best suit their needs and will take considerable trouble to find a specialist breeder either through the Dog Directory, the canine press or the Kennel Club. There is no doubt in my mind that a dog's first home is its best home and that means the direct sale of puppies by the breeder to the family which is going to feed, train and keep the dog throughout its life. The responsible breeder takes great pains to ensure that the home to which their puppy is being sold is suitable in every way and this means advertising, time, trouble and expense. There is a temptation to arrange the sale of whole or part of a litter to a trading kennel but, apart from the objections outlined already, much of the pleasure of breeding well-reared and sound stock is lost if you do not keep some sort of track of your extended family. Christmas is a particularly happy time for us because so many of our puppy owners send a card and, often, a photograph of the dog and news of its progress. Owners frequently telephone with a problem (fortunately, usually minor) and this is also an occasion which enables us to keep track.

Breeders themselves are sometimes full-time professionals (often with a boarding kennel or trimming and grooming business) breeding just for sale – although if the job is to be done properly there is not a great deal of profit in it – but, increasingly, they are breeding to improve or replace their own dogs as companions and/or for work or show. Inevitably, they have a surplus and it is these well-bred puppies which make the most suitable family pets. As well as the serious breeders there are the one-bitch families who feel that they would like a puppy from their bitch and who, perhaps,

Sticks taste delicious – but they should be discouraged

want to introduce their children to the wonder and mystery of birth in a practical and sensible way. (Others take such an opportunity if it is offered by way of a misalliance!) These bitches are not necessarily of known pedigree but there is no reason why the puppies should not be healthy and sound and good homes can still be found. Indeed many people believe that a crossbred dog is more healthy than one with a pedigree. This is simply not true. Just to set the record straight: firstly, the consequence of too close linebreeding can, and does, occasionally lead to complications. The breeds in which these occur are few but any good reference book on dog breeds or specialist breed books almost always describe them, their frequency and their seriousness. Secondly, the purchase of a pedigree puppy enables the purchaser to know, in advance, the shape and the size of an adult dog and to know the characteristics which are to be expected. Thirdly, in the case of most mongrel litters the sire is unknown and he is most likely to be the leader of the local feral pack (ie the most aggressive, the biggest and least responsive of those dogs which stray or are rejected by their owners) rather than a well-bred, properly adjusted family pet. Incidentally, the term 'mongrel' implies a dog bred from crossbred or mongrel parents while the term 'crossbred' usually means that the sire and the dam were of known pedigree.

Whatever the circumstances, breeding one litter in a lifetime is just as serious a business for dog and owner as the breeding of several litters a year. So, although this book is primarily for those who are becoming or would like to become serious breeders of dogs, I hope that it will also be a useful and essentially practical reference work for anyone who would like to breed from their bitch.

I have tried to make available to you the best possible advice, information and encouragement and where my own qualifications are less than adequate I have persuaded experts in their respective fields to make a contribution. Their expertise adds greatly to the value of this work and I am much indebted to them for their chapters and their advice. I am also indebted to the veterinary surgeons, friends and, most of all to my dogs, who over the years have taught me so much. If anybody is to be mentioned by name they must be Mrs Moira Burden of the Cressex Golden Retrievers, Miss Margaret Barnes of the Suntop English Setters and Dr Peter Larkin MRCVS. Their advice, patience and assistance have been absolutely invaluable.

1 First Steps

Deliberately arranging the creation of a new being, particularly one which is so dependent on the whims and fashions of Man, is a very great responsibility. Please do not embark on this enterprise unless you are quite sure that you are able to rear the puppies properly, ensure that your bitch gets the extra food and attention she will need, pay for the veterinary fees if required, house the bitch and the puppies properly and find responsible owners when they are old enough. Breeding dogs is not something that can be done on the cheap. From the cost of the stud fee to the advertising expenses for the sale of puppies you will be paying out, and there is no return at all for four months or so. Even then you might well not cover your expenses. You also have a moral responsibility beyond the sale of the puppies. Their owners will telephone you with their problems – which they will expect you to be able to solve – and, on occasions, they may even have to give up the dog altogether because of illness, bereavement or emigration. I hope that this helps you to realise that breeding from your bitch is not to be undertaken lightly. However, if you are determined to go ahead you will need:

ENERGY

Breeding is hard work if you are going to do the job properly. Although things usually go quite smoothly, there is an unavoidable background of concern which contributes to a certain amount of stress. I hope this book will prevent your being plagued by persistent and nagging worry as this can and does communicate itself to the bitch and make her nervous. But concern there will be and, if you are the worrying kind, this can sap at your reserves of energy. It is hard, physical work as well. A litter of ten can have you on your feet from morning till night during weaning and early rearing. By the time you have prepared food, fed puppies, cleaned up and had a cup of tea it's almost time to start all over again. And do not forget that your normal life must go on as well. For many this involves a home, a family and, perhaps, other dogs. Few can organise things in such a way that they have a holiday after the last pup has been sold – but I can assure you that you will feel as if you need one!

Puppies are also the best time-wasters in the world so things that can be left until later tend to get left – and then you have it all to do at once. But the work is well rewarded when you can take a break and watch the pups at play – a time when you can enjoy yourself as well as helping them to become 'socialised'. This, of course, leaves even less time for all the other things and, when they finally settle down to a well-deserved sleep, you find that you are busy ironing or doing your accounts!

A Sound and Healthy Bitch

Your breeding bitch is the subject of a later chapter but, for the moment, let me emphasise the importance of health, fitness and temperament. No bitch should be bred from if she is not sound. She should be strong, lean, able to go on a really good walk without returning out of breath and tired and have the sparkle and 'bloom' that comes with good health. Incidentally, some of the brachycephalic breeds are naturally rather 'snuffly' but they should still be able to exert themselves without discomfort. Any particular weakness in eye, muzzle, rib cage, back or hips should be the subject of very careful assessment before the bitch is brought to stud. Exactly where the line should be drawn between what is and what is not acceptable will necessarily be the subject of differences of opinion. The safest course is that if you are finding it difficult to make up your mind about a particular mating then you should not go ahead.

Temperament is also of vital importance, and when discussing temperament we are not just talking of dogs who are aggressive. We have a bitch who, now that she has reached middle age and is somewhat calmer than she once was, has been a very worthy champion. She would not harm a soul but as a youngster she drove us mad. She would escape from anywhere, she would dig franticly and senselessly, bark at anything that moved (and some things that didn't) and howl in anguish whenever the telephone rang. It would not have been fair to prospective owners to sell her puppies so we have never bred from her.

We shall see where that black eye came from later

A Sound and Healthy Sire

Much of what has been said of the bitch also applies to the dog. However, there is one important difference: the number of puppies a bitch will whelp during her lifetime is limited whereas the number of puppies a popular dog can sire may run into hundreds. This means that any fault in the sire has many more times the chance of being passed on through his progeny than a fault in the bitch, so that if the selection of a brood bitch is important then the selection of a stud dog is even more so. We shall be discussing the 'gene pool' in a later chapter but, for the present, let me emphasise the importance of a prospective stud dog's ability to sire quality puppies. The greatest dogs have not always been the best sires and, in fact, it is more important to assess the progeny of a dog or bitch than it is for the sire or the dam to have won lots of first prizes or Challenge Certificates.

Time

I would not go so far as to say that it is impossible to breed a litter of puppies if you have anything else to do on a regular basis, but the more you have to do the more difficult it becomes to do the job properly. Certainly, to hold down a regular job that takes you away from home for any length of time should preclude you from even considering breeding. It is absolutely essential that you should be free to attend to your bitch and her litter exactly when that attention is required. For four to five weeks after whelping you will have your hands very full indeed and there should be nothing to prevent you from giving all the time that is needed to the litter.

Premises

Bitches behave very differently during whelping. Some are quite happy to have their puppies in the kitchen with all and sundry tramping through the room although most like much more privacy. I do think it is important that you have an area you can set aside and keep secluded so that your bitch can be left in peace. It must be a place which you can easily keep very warm and which is relatively quiet, although still within hearing range of the sounds which the bitch is used to. The best place, of course, is where the bitch normally sleeps but for many people this is either outside in kennels which cannot be economically heated or a kitchen which is too noisy and busy.

Whatever you decide, do alter the sleeping arrangements for your bitch three or four weeks before she is due to whelp. There can be nothing worse than being comfortably settled and then being shifted into strange and unusual surroundings just before the event. Your bitch will already be restless enough during the few days before whelping without her having to cope with an unfamiliar environment. It is very difficult to lay down hard and fast rules because circumstances range from purpose-built kennels to a spare bedroom. However, if you keep the bitch's comfort and welfare in mind rather than your own convenience you should not go far wrong! Incidentally, if you have more than two bitches you use for breeding you will need a breeder's licence which will be granted by your local authority. A form is obtainable from the planning department and they will probably send someone round to inspect the premises to see that these are suitable.

THE WHELPING BOX

The basic requirements of the whelping box are fairly simple. It should be plenty big enough for the bitch to stretch out, turn round and stand up, remembering that she will have to be able to do this after her puppies are born without treading all over them. The box should be covered but have a lid that can be lifted so that you can see inside without disturbing her, it should have an entrance just large enough for her to be able to get in and out easily and it should be very well insulated.

Figure 1 Whelping box

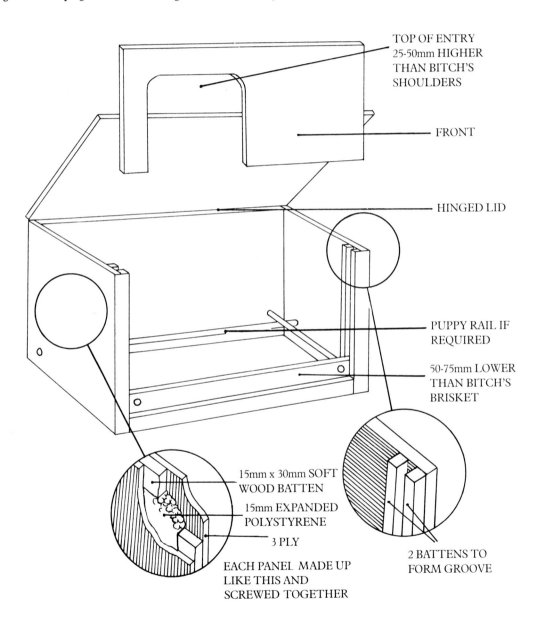

TOP OF ENTRY 25-50mm HIGHER THAN BITCH'S SHOULDERS

FRONT

HINGED LID

PUPPY RAIL IF REQUIRED

50-75mm LOWER THAN BITCH'S BRISKET

15mm x 30mm SOFT WOOD BATTEN

15mm EXPANDED POLYSTYRENE

3 PLY

EACH PANEL MADE UP LIKE THIS AND SCREWED TOGETHER

2 BATTENS TO FORM GROOVE

Figure 1 shows the construction of a type which I have been using for some years and is self-explanatory. It has the advantage that it is very adaptable; as the pups grow the section in which the entrance is cut can be turned upside down so that they cannot get out. The sliding pieces at the front also enable you to clean it out easily. If the bitch is one of the larger breeds (Irish Wolfhound or Great Dane) or is very heavy in relation to her size (Boxer or Bull Terrier), it is sensible to insert a rail to prevent the pups being crushed by the bitch. Exactly where it is placed will depend on the size of the breed but it should be in a position which allows the puppies to slide underneath it easily up until they are about two weeks old. I do not think that this precaution is necessary with most breeds – puppies are pretty tough!

Make sure that you have the whelping box thoroughly cleaned and disinfected well before the date of whelping. It should be available when you move the bitch into her whelping quarters so that she has time to get used to it.

There are many opinions about the best method of keeping the puppies warm. I believe that, except for some of the smaller, smooth-coated breeds, the best solution is a well-insulated whelping box in a warm room. If the bitch and her puppies are bedded on several layers of newspapers with SnugRug or other suitable fur fabric on top then quite enough heat will be generated for the puppies to be comfortable. I do not like the use of infra-red lamps for puppies; for one thing the heat generated is very drying and, for another, the bitch can easily become far too hot and have to leave the whelping box to be comfortable. I also think most bitches like to have privacy during their confinement and a lamp necessitates leaving the top of the box open all the time. If you feel that you do need to heat the whelping box the best method is to use one of the flat heating pads which are simply plugged into a convenient plug. It is essential to ensure that the cable goes through the floor of the whelping box so that it cannot be nibbled by inquisitive puppies or anxious bitches. This is a much better arrangement than the traditional hot-water bottle wrapped in a blanket.

It is well worth spending some time and trouble on constructing a really good whelping box. For the price of a couple of sheets of plywood, a few feet of 50mm section softwood and a couple of dozen ceiling tiles you can gain considerable peace of mind knowing that come cold weather or power cuts your bitch and her litter will be warm and snug. A well-made box will last for years so it is a very worthwhile investment.

A VETERINARY SURGEON

It is probable that you already have a veterinary surgeon with whom you have formed a working relationship but it is as well to talk to him or her well before your bitch's litter is due. Some veterinary surgeons prefer not to be committed to possible whelping complications and this is particularly so in the one-man practices. The reason is that the vet may find himself involved for several hours and therefore unable to deal with other emergencies which may occur at the same time. So make sure that your vet knows the approximate date the litter is due and that he is willing to help should help be required. If you do not have your own vet ask around in your area about the practices – the local dog training club is a good place to start. Not all vets are sympathetic to dog breeders so it is as well to find one that understands their special requirements. I believe that the relationship you form with your vet is very important, both for your peace of mind and for the comfort of your bitch. Someone sensible and calm – and in my experience most vets are – can be distinctly advantageous when your bitch has been pushing for two hours and you are running round in small circles at three o'clock in the morning.

TRANSPORT

I give a special heading to this because many people do not realise how vital it can be. Unless your vet lives next door a car or van is absolutely essential. In the event of any difficulties it will be necessary for you to move the bitch rather than for the vet to come to you. It is possible that an injection or manipulation will solve the problem but, if it does not, then you are going to have to go to the surgery anyway.

A caesarean is too complicated an operation to be carried out on your kitchen table! It is possible to do it, of course, but the chances of success are much greater if all the right equipment is near at hand. The same applies if there are any complications later with the bitch or the puppies – the faster you can get to the vet the more likely you are to save a life. Transport may not always be necessary; with radio control and all the rest of it your vet may be able to get to you more quickly, especially during the day. But it is not worth the risk of not having your own transport. Make sure that your car has been serviced well before the litter is due and, if necessary, make your husband go to work on his bicycle for a couple of weeks so that you can have the car!

MONEY

It is very difficult to work out how much money you will need to have available because there are so many factors to be taken into consideration. At the best end of the scale is the medium-sized, easy-whelping bitch of a breed which tends to have small litters. At the other end is the large breed likely to whelp twelve or fifteen puppies – some of which might still require care and feeding when they are much older than eight weeks because they are difficult to sell! My own bitches are at the happier end of the spectrum but I do not feel comfortable unless I have about twice the going rate for a puppy of the breed available against expenses and emergencies. A good rule of thumb is to work out how much it costs to feed your bitch under normal circumstances in a week and then multiply this sum by one hundred. This is about what you will need for the stud fee, basic veterinary care, food, pills, powders and potions for the bitch and her puppies from the time of mating until the puppies are sold. You should add to this sum a few pounds for advertising and should be prepared for the cost of a caesarean. Naturally, a stud fee does not have to be taken into account if the bitch is crossbred or mismated, but all the other expenses remain the same. Of course, this outlay is spread over a period of about four months so you may have enough left over from your 'normal' expenditure. Anyway it is not so important how your expenses are accommodated so long as you realise that they exist, and that if you are going to breed healthy puppies those bills will have to be met. Petplan have recently introduced a scheme which includes cover for brood bitches.

This four-week-old
puppy does not look
much like a Welsh Corgi.
Many of the prick-eared
breeds take some time to
realise that their ears
should be held up

For the serious breeder more details will be discussed in the later chapter on records and paperwork but mention must be made of the financial aspects now as in some circumstances — the case of a mongrel litter, for instance, where the puppies will inevitably realise a very low figure, — it will be quite impossible to recoup the total outlay.

OTHER USEFUL ITEMS

1 As much good-quality newspaper as you can gather − remember to choose your daily paper with care as some are much less suitable than others. Broadsheet is best and of these I have found that the Telegraph and the Financial Times are best. Some of the Sundays are good but don't bother to save the Sunday Times or the Radio or TV Times. Small or non-absorbent sheets are a complete waste of time!

2 Two good-quality polyester fibre blankets − I consider SnugRug to be the best but there are others on the market. These blankets are absolutely safe for bitch and puppies, are easily washable, dry quickly and stay dry on their surface. But most important − they are warm and they stay warm!

3 First-aid kit consisting of:

Disposable surgical gloves

Several pieces of boiled, rough towelling

Large, clean sheet

Glucose
Ear dropper
Premature baby's bottle and teats or a kitten bottle
Carton of dried milk formulated for puppies (Whelpi, Lactol or similar)
Tube of KY surgical jelly – you can use Petroleum Jelly or Vaseline but they are rather messy. The KY is water soluble and can be washed off easily
Small pair of curved surgical scissors
Dettol or other good-quality disinfectant
Artery forceps – particularly if you have one of the larger breeds
Brandy – a drop for the bitch, a puppy or yourself can work wonders! (Brandy given to dogs *must* be diluted with an equal quantity of water)

I hope that this is essentially a practical book but I do think that the practical details are much more relevant if one understands some of the theory which lies behind the technique. For this reason I feel that it would be sensible to study the dog and the bitch in detail and to learn a little, or brush up on, some basic genetics before we get round to discussing the actual mating, whelping and weaning. You may feel that you can skip these chapters and you might be right, but I learned a great deal in their compilation which I had not realised that I did not know. I hope you will find the same.

2 Introduction to Genetics

by Dr Heather Pidduck
LECTURER IN GENETICS AT THE ROYAL VETERINARY
COLLEGE, LONDON

Genetics is a fascinating and challenging subject. Some of the theory is quite difficult but, once understood, it can be put to considerable practical use in the breeding of pedigree dogs. In this short chapter I have tried to cover four basic areas: the physical nature of the genetic material; its transmission from parents to offspring: its expression or manifestation; and the manipulation of the genetic material by the breeder in his or her choice of breeding system.

The Physical Nature of the Genetic Material – Genes and Chromosomes

The chromosomes are fine, threadlike structures present in every body cell. Each chromosome carries genetic material as a sequence of genes which are coded instructions specifying the genetic blueprint of the individual. In each body cell in the dog there are thirty-nine different chromosomes, each with a specific but different selection of genes. An average length chromosome probably carries between fifty and two hundred genes. Every cell contains two copies of each chromosome, thus each cell has $2 \times 39 = 78$ chromosomes. Seventy-eight is called the *diploid number*. A diagrammatic representation of the chromosomes in the dog is shown in Figure 2.

It can be seen that in both sexes all but two of the chromosomes form identical pairs (the autosomes), but the thirty-ninth pair (the sex chromosomes) is identical only in

Figure 2 Diagrammatic representation of the chromosomes of the dog

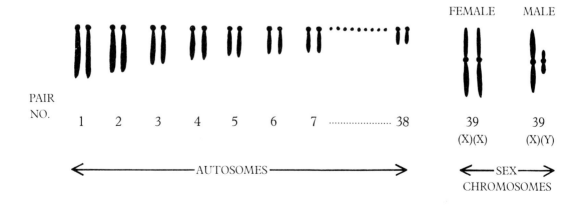

| PAIR NO. | 1 | 2 | 3 | 4 | 5 | 6 | 7 | .... | 38 | FEMALE 39 (X)(X) | MALE 39 (X)(Y) |

←————————— AUTOSOMES —————————→   ←— SEX —→ CHROMOSOMES

the female, being a pair of X chromosomes, but distinct in the male, being an X and a Y chromosome.

The chromosome set is species specific and thus all dogs, whatever their breed, have an identical chromosome picture, with a diploid number of seventy-eight. The obvious physical diversity of such breeds as the Chihuahua, the Great Dane, the Dalmation and the Poodle is controlled by invisible differences in the chemical formulae of the genes. Wolves also have seventy-eight chromosomes which are very similar in shape and size to the diploid set of the dog – a finding which supports the close evolutionary proximity of wolves and dogs. (The two species will in fact interbreed.) Humans have a diploid number of forty-six, great apes forty-eight, cattle sixty, cats thirty-eight, donkeys sixty-two and horses sixty-four. In all mammals the chromosomal distinction of the sexes is the same, females being XX and males XY. The X chromosome is generally one of the largest in the set and the Y generally the smallest. For all that, the Y is very strongly male determining.

The Transmission of the Genetic Material

There are two types of cell division: the first type is the one involved in the continuous replacement of body cells such as skin cells in healing. This is a very simple division; an exact copy of each of the seventy-eight chromosomes and other cell inclusions is made and the 'doubled' cell then divides into two cells each with the full diploid number of chromosomes.

The second type of division is restricted to reproductive organs and is responsible for the production of *gametes* (eggs in the bitch and sperm in the dog). If gametes were produced which each contained seventy-eight chromosomes, then at fertilisation a *double diploid* embryo would be produced with one hundred and fifty-six chromosomes! Therefore, in the production of eggs and sperm a reduction division occurs, such that each gamete produced contains just one member of each chromosome pair, the diploid number is therefore halved, or becomes *haploid*. Fertilisation of a haploid egg (39) by a haploid sperm (39) then restores the diploid number (78) in the embryo.

It is by the processes of reduction division and fertilisation that the genes get reassorted in two ways: firstly, in the reduction division there is a pairing and exchange of segments between identical chromosome pairs. Since one member of each chromosome pair is of maternal origin and the other of paternal origin this means that there are new parental combinations of genes in the gametes. (Fig. 3)

Secondly, since only one member of each chromosome pair goes into each gamete, and since which one goes in is purely chance, there must almost be an infinite number of different chromosome combinations in the gametes. In other words, every time an animal reproduces it passes on fifty per cent of its genetic blueprint, but that fifty per cent is unique to each offspring (except in the case of identical twins).

But how is the sex of each offspring determined? The reduction division involves the sex chromosomes as well as the autosomes. Therefore, when an XX cell divides, in the production of eggs in the bitch, each of the eggs produced being haploid will have thirty-eight autosomes and a single X chromosome. But reduction division of an

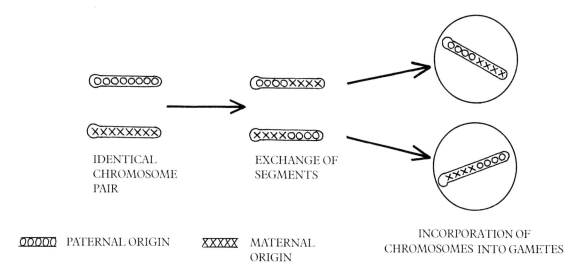

IDENTICAL
CHROMOSOME
PAIR

EXCHANGE OF
SEGMENTS

INCORPORATION OF
CHROMOSOMES INTO GAMETES

ꙨꙨꙨꙨꙨ PATERNAL ORIGIN   XXXXX MATERNAL
ORIGIN

XY cell will lead to fifty per cent of sperms having an X chromosome and the other fifty per cent having a Y chromosome. So approximately half of fertilisations will be X egg with X sperm, and the other half X egg with Y sperm leading to the production of equal numbers of female (XX) and male (XY) puppies. In a litter of only two or three it frequently happens, by chance, that all puppies are of one sex, but when you add in other litters you will find that the sex ratio does come out at 50:50. There is nothing you can do to change it, mating a bitch early or late in her season has no influence whatsoever. If there was a method of distorting the sex ratio in animals, dairy cattle breeders would certainly have taken advantage of it!

Figure 3 The incorporation of chromosomes into gametes

The Expression or Manifestation of the Genetic Material

We now know the physical form that the genetic material takes and how it is passed from the parents to their offspring. Next, we need to know how the genetic material is expressed. It is convenient to look separately at characteristics which are under single-gene control, and those influenced by more than one gene. Then we will be in a position to understand the pros and cons of different breeding systems.

CHARACTERISTICS CONTROLLED BY SINGLE GENES

Each gene, as described earlier, is at a fixed chromosomal position and is a coded instruction for making a particular product. For example, there is an autosomal gene, B, which is just one of many involved in the control of coat colour in the dog (other genes are responsible for whether or not pigment shall be made, its intensity and its distribution − whether in spots, patches or solid colour etc). The B gene controls only the base colour of the pigment synthesised. There are two varieties of the gene − B and b. Different varieties, or alleles, can be thought of as different instructions: B is an instruction to make black pigment, b is an instruction to make brown (liver) pigment. So a dog, having two sites for this gene because the chromosomes are paired, can have the genotype BB, Bb or bb. If both alleles are the same, that is BB or bb, we say that the genotype is *homozygous*. Where the alleles differ, Bb, the genotype is *heterozygous*. However, one B allele is sufficient to result in black pigment and masks the b allele, if present, so the genotypes BB and Bb look identical, that is they have an identical black phenotype and the bb genotype has a brown phenotype. The B allele is thus called dominant and b recessive. This explains why some black dogs only pass on black but others pass on black and brown. The former must be homozygous BB and the latter heterozygous Bb. Of course, brown, bb, can only pass on brown.

For some genes there is no dominance and so we can distinguish the heterozygote from both homozygotes. An example is M, merle, another gene involved in coat colour. Homozygous (MM) individuals are white, deaf and blind, heterozygous (Mm) individuals have merle coat colour and wall eyes and homozygous (mm) individuals are non-merle, their colour being determined by their other coat colour genes. Thus, we can predict what will happen if two merle dogs are mated (each has the genotype Mm and thus produces equal proportions of M and m bearing gametes).

We can set this out as a square, with contributions from the bitch across the top and from the dog down the side:

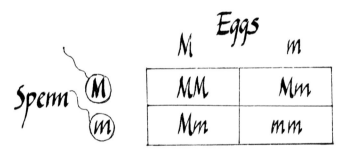

The offspring will therefore comprise one quarter MM (white, deaf and blind), half Mm (merle) and a quarter mm (non-merle). Clearly, we will not always get these exact proportions (1:2:1) because of chance* but overall this will be the ratio obtained. So, a breeder who mates merle with merle must expect roughly a quarter of the offspring to be deaf and blind and only one half of the offspring to show the merle colour of the parents. However, a mating of Merle (Mm) to non-merle (mm) will result in equal numbers of merle and non-merle offspring thus avoiding the production of unwanted MM puppies.

The ratio of 1:2:1 of genotypes is very important and it is seen as a 3:1 phenotypic ratio where one allele is dominant and one is recessive. We can see this if we return to the example of the B locus. If we cross two heterozygous black individuals, three quarters of the offspring will be black (BB, Bb, Bb) and a quarter brown (bb). This is the 3:1 ratio.

---

*A coin would be expected to land heads and tails with equal frequency, but you would not be surprised if in six tosses you obtained four heads and two tails.

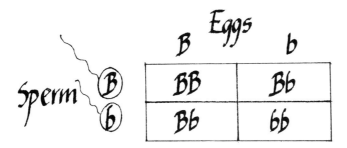

We have no way of knowing which of the black puppies are BB and which Bb unless we test mate them, by crossing them with homozygous recessive brown (bb). If a black dog has the genotype BB, then when crossed with bb all the offspring will be black (Bb):

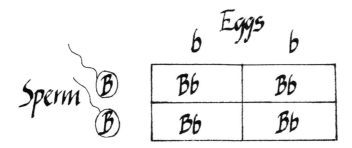

But, if the black dog is Bb then the cross with bb will produce a litter with equal numbers of brown and black puppies:

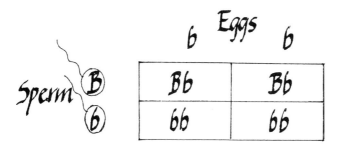

You may have come across a form of test mating to check a prospective stud dog for heterozygosity for an abnormality caused by a single gene. One of the best examples is Progressive Retinal Atrophy (PRA) which in many, but not all, breeds is caused by homozygosity for an autosomal recessive gene. Thus, if we call the abnormal allele p and the normal allele P our suspected individual is either homozygous normal PP or heterozygous normal Pp, often called a carrier.

For the purpose of test mating we would ideally mate him with a bitch that was homozygous (pp) (ie a bitch with PRA). Then if the sire were clear (PP) none of the puppies would develop PRA but if he were a carrier (Pp) half the puppies would be expected to develop PRA.

In some cases it is not possible to do this classical form of test mating, and a heterozygous bitch or bitches must be used (detected by their own breeding records). Then if the sire were clear (PP) the mating (PP x Pp) would produce all phenotypically normal offspring but if he were a carrier (Pp) we would expect three normal to one PRA. Obviously, if there were four normal puppies this would not prove anything − but what if there were eight in the litter, all normal? The answer is that, in this case, by declaring him clear there would be a one in ten chance that you were wrong. In Table 1 these chances of being wrong are given for three different types of test mating, so you can see just how difficult it can be to be reasonably sure that an animal is not carrying a particular recessive allele.

Table 1 CHANCES OF BEING WRONG.

(The author is grateful to W.G. Hill for his help in preparing this table.)

Tables giving the chances of *not* detecting that an individual is heterozygous for a particular autosomal recessive gene.

1 By mating the suspect individual to known homozygous recessives (ie mating to individuals *showing* the condition).

	C H A N C E		
	1 in 10	1 in 20	1 in 100
Numbers of offspring required *not* showing the condition (N)	4	5	7

Explanation: If the suspect *is* heterozygous then, when mated to affected homozygotes, there is a 1 in 10 chance of 4 normal offspring, a 1 in 20 chance of 5 normal offspring and only a 1 in 100 chance of 7 normal offspring. Therefore, the chances of you being wrong, in declaring the suspect clear are correspondingly 1 in 10 (4 normals), 1 in 20 (5 normals) and 1 in 100 (7 normals). In other words, the more normal individuals produced, the less the chance of you being wrong in declaring a suspect clear.

2 By mating the suspect individual to known heterozygotes (ie mating to individuals *carrying* the condition.)

	C H A N C E		
	1 in 10	1 in 20	1 in 100
N	8	11	16

3 By mating the suspect individual to his or her offspring (which if the suspect *is* heterozygous means that his offspring have a one in two chance of being heterozygous). Litter size is significant here.

	C H A N C E		
	1 in 10	1 in 20	1 in 100
Litter size	*Numbers of litters needed*		
1	18	23	35
2	10	13	19
3	7	9	14
4	6	8	12
5	5	7	10
6	5	6	9
7	5	6	9
8	4	6	8
10	4	5	8
12	4	5	7
∞	4	5	7

Explanation: For example, where the breed averages a litter size of five. If the suspect *is* heterozygous, then, when mated to one of his offspring, there is a 1 in 10 chance of all members being normal in five litters, a 1 in 20 chance for 7 litters and a 1 in 100 chance for 10 litters. Therefore, the chance of you being wrong in declaring your suspect clear on the basis of 5, 7 and 10 all normal litters is 1 in 10, 1 in 20 and 1 in 100.

Clearly, test mating schemes require considerable organisation as well as co-operation within a breed society. Additionally, one needs to be sure that the condition is caused by homozygosity for an autosomal recessive.

Figure 4 shows a pedigree of German Shepherd Dogs where a recessive dwarfing gene is present. Four of the litters with affected members can be traced back to a common sire or grandsire and all could probably be shown to be related, if the pedigree data were complete. Recessive inheritance is typified by a sporadic occurrence, the abnormality generally occurring most frequently where parents are closely related. For an abnormality of unknown cause the first step must be to determine whether or not the abnormality is inherited. One of the simplest ways is to mate the affected individual with one of its parents. If there are affected individuals in the resultant litter then the condition is probably inherited (there will, of course, be exceptions, when all members of a kennel are exposed to a common infectious agent). If reasonable numbers of puppies are produced, none of whom are affected, then you may be able to refute any genetic cause and continue your breeding plans undaunted. If transmission of the disorder behaves as an autosomal recessive and you want to minimise its future occurrence then you must: (1) Never breed from affected animals. (2) *Either* check by test mating all your suspected carrier males and only continue your line with proven clear sires *or* use for breeding only those males which have no affected parents, offspring or litter mates.

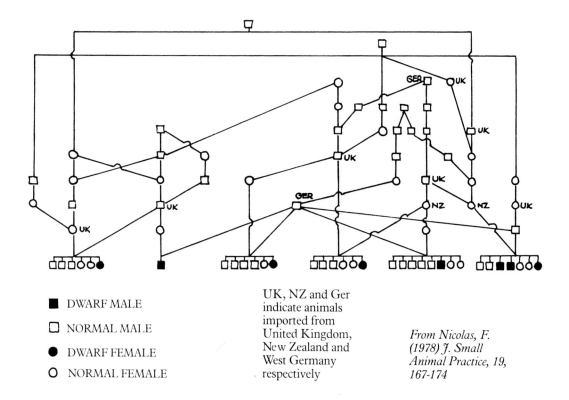

■ DWARF MALE

□ NORMAL MALE

● DWARF FEMALE

○ NORMAL FEMALE

UK, NZ and Ger
indicate animals
imported from
United Kingdom,
New Zealand and
West Germany
respectively

*From Nicolas, F.
(1978) J. Small
Animal Practice, 19,
167-174*

Figure 4 Transmission of an autosomal recessive disorder. Dwarfism in a German Shepherd pedigree

With either of these methods you will reduce the incidence of the abnormality but you will not eliminate the abnormal allele because of the absence of selection against carriers on the female side. Of prime importance is honesty both with yourself and with other breeders. Removing one or two puppies with a known recessive abnormality by culling at birth may be widely practised and even reasonable, but in rearing the remaining healthy litter mates and perhaps subsequent sale and breeding you must never forget that they may be heterozygous and perpetuate the disorder.

This section on single gene effects would be incomplete without brief mention of the transmission of autosomal dominant and sex-linked disorders. An abnormality caused by a dominant allele is easily recognised in a pedigree and simple to eradicate because all individuals with the allele manifest the condition. There is no skipping of generations as there is with recessives. Figure 5 shows a pedigree of a dominant disorder.

Sex-linked characteristics are those which are controlled by genes present on the X chromosome. They are not characteristics which distinguish the sexes. The only gene yet identified on the X chromosome in the dog is that for haemophilia. All members of the vast majority of breeds have the dominant allele (H) for normal blood clotting.

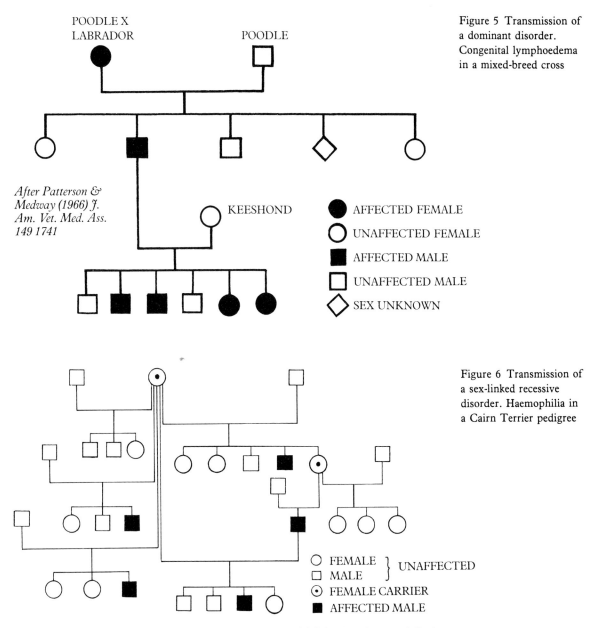

Figure 5 Transmission of a dominant disorder. Congenital lymphoedema in a mixed-breed cross

After Patterson & Medway (1966) J. Am. Vet. Med. Ass. 149 1741

- ● AFFECTED FEMALE
- ○ UNAFFECTED FEMALE
- ■ AFFECTED MALE
- □ UNAFFECTED MALE
- ◇ SEX UNKNOWN

Figure 6 Transmission of a sex-linked recessive disorder. Haemophilia in a Cairn Terrier pedigree

- ○ FEMALE ⎫ UNAFFECTED
- □ MALE ⎭
- ⊙ FEMALE CARRIER
- ■ AFFECTED MALE

In a handful of breeds an abnormal recessive allele (h) which leads to haemophilia has been reported in just a few individuals. Figure 6 shows a pedigree of Cairn Terriers where some members are affected with haemophilia.

Because h is recessive and on the X chromosome, the posssession of one normal dominant allele, H, confers normality. Since males have only one X chromosome, if this carries the abnormal allele (h) then haemophilia results. Females, having two X chromosomes, are only affected if they are hh, having inherited an abnormal allele both from an affected father and from an affected or carrier mother. Since this is a highly unlikely mating, haemophiliacs are invariably male as are all sufferers from X-linked recessive disorders (in Man haemophilia, colour blindness and certain forms of muscular dystrophy are all X-linked).

CHARACTERISTICS INFLUENCED BY MORE THAN ONE GENE

We are now in a position to look at a subject called *polygenic inheritance*. The term 'polygenic' means just what it says, that is many genes influencing the expression of one characteristic. Frequently, polygenically controlled characteristics are also affected by environmental influences, such as feeding, exercise and training. This is in contrast to most characteristics controlled by single genes, such as coat and eye colour and abnormalities like dwarfism and PRA. However you feed and exercise a genetically black dog it will remain black and no amount of feeding will change a genetically dwarf animal to one of normal stature.

Characteristics under polygenic control are such quantitative characteristics as weight, height, temperament and number of puppies in a litter. All of these show continuous variation from one extreme to the other with most individuals in the middle or average. If, for example, we measure the mature height in any breed of dog, we would find, in addition to the difference between dogs and bitches, that the heights would fall in a distribution something like Figure 7.

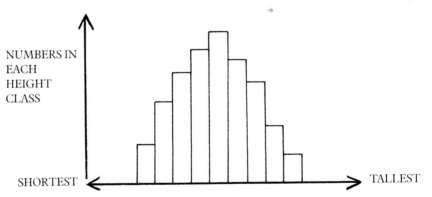

NUMBERS IN EACH HEIGHT CLASS

SHORTEST   TALLEST

Figure 7 Pattern of mature height

There are two genetic aspects of this which are important: the first is the kind of genetic control which is responsible, the second is the proportional contribution of genetic and non-genetic influences. Let us examine this as two questions:

1 What kind of genetic control is responsible?

First let's look at single-gene control. If we have a gene H with two alternative alleles H^+ and H^-, the H^+ leading to increased height and H^- leading to decreased height, then we would have a maximum of three phenotypes: tall (H^+H^+) medium (H^+H^-) and short (H^-H^-). Clearly, the members of a dog breed cannot be classified as tall, medium and short so single-gene control cannot be responsible. What about two genes? Gene H_1 and H_2 and each with + and − alternatives. This gives us far more variety. Every dog must have two alleles of H_1 and two alleles of H_2. So each can have in total anything from none to four $+$ alleles:

ie $- - - -$ $- - - +$ $- - + +$ $- + + +$ $+ + + +$

So if there is no dominance and if a $+$ allele of the H_1 gene contributes the same to height (say, ½ cm) as a $+$ allele of the H_2 gene (similarly with the $-$ alleles) there will be five different genotypes. Clearly, identical genotypes do not always result in identical phenotypes (if they did how could we explain the small differences between human identical twin pairs who differ on average by 1.7 cm in height?). So we can imagine that our simple two-gene theory could quite well account for the range of heights we observe within one breed. We call these genes *polygenes* and although individually they have very small effect, combined they are powerful. This is the simplest possible model of polygenic inheritance. It will become more complex with (a) an increase in the number of genes involved, (b) dominance and (c) variable contributions from different genes. It is envisaged that these polygenes do not necessarily directly affect height, for instance a gene influencing the rate of bone growth and a gene influencing the production of growth hormone will both contribute to adult height.

Equally important is the fact that genes are unlikely to have individual and separate effects. A gene concerned with the rate of bone growth is likely to also influence the formation of hip and shoulder joints, and a gene influencing growth hormone production could also affect the age and weight at which sexual maturity is reached. In other words, we should appreciate that the finished product, ie the dog or bitch, is a manifestation of a complex interaction of all the genes within the genotype, and non-genetic influences which will now be explained.

Obviously we can predict, with reasonable accuracy, the height of offspring from a particular mating. For instance, if we mate a larger-than-average bitch and dog, we will generally get larger-than-average puppies, but sometimes we will get average or even smaller-than-average puppies. This is because there are also non-genetic influences (environmental influences) on quantitative characteristics. The determination of adult size begins very early in embryonic life. The position of the embryo in the uterus and the size of the uterus both have some prenatal influence on final skeletal size, whatever the genotype for size. How well the bitch nourishes the pups both before and after birth is also a very important environmental influence. So some large adult individuals may be the manifestation of a 'large' genotype in an average environment, but others may be the product of an 'average' genotype which has benefited from an optimal environment.

We now have an answer to the question, what kind of genetic control is responsible, the answer being: a number of genes with individually small effect are responsible, and their expression is subject to interaction with other genes and modification by a variety of environmental influences. The word *multifactorial* is often used as it encompasses both polygenic and environmental contributions.

2 How much of the variation in a quantitative characteristic is due to genetic and how much is due to environmental influence?

The answer to this question is given by the *heritability* of the characteristic. Heritability is a measure (expressed as a percentage) of the proportion of the variation in a quantitative characteristic which is due to genetic variation. The mathematics are complicated and need not concern us, but an understanding of the meaning of heritability is essential. It is perhaps the most misunderstood and misused term in genetics and so its explanation deserves some space.

Reference to two hypothetical examples, one of low and one of high heritability, should help. Say we find that the heritability of obedience in a particular working breed of dogs is 10 per cent. This means that of the variation measured in obedience between dogs in the breed, 10 per cent is due to variation in genetic makeup and 90 per cent to variation in environmental origin (eg the skill of the trainer(s), the age at which training begins, the incentives and rewards, the social structure of the animal groupings, etc). In other words, a heritability for obedience of 10 per cent means that obedient dogs are primarily the result of training rather than of breeding. This is not necessarily true of other breeds − heritability estimates are specific to the individuals providing the information on which the estimate is based, but a value for one breed is often a very useful guide to another breed.

Mature height is an example of a quantitative characteristic which has high heritability (probably around 60 − 70 per cent in most breeds). In other words, the height variation which exists within a breed is about 60 − 70 per cent accountable to variation in genetic makeup and only 30 − 40 per cent accountable to variation in feeding and other aspects of the environment. The consequence is that should we wish to increase or decrease the height standard in a breed, then the genetic variation is available to make this possible, within reasonable limits. By breeding from animals who are the tallest (or shortest) in the breed the breed average will gradually increase (or decrease). This does *not* mean that the genetic potential is there for the production of miniatures or giants of each breed. Such extremes are generally controlled by single genes and are known in only a limited selection of breeds.

A discussion of heritability would be incomplete without mentioning the heritability of various abnormalities. PRA, as discussed earlier, is caused in most breeds by a single gene and is not influenced by environment. So, in that sense, the variation between individuals regarding the presence or absence of PRA is entirely of genetic origin, so we could say that the heritability of PRA is one hundred per cent. (Note that heritabilities are usually only calculated for quantitative characteristics.) At the other extreme, in an outbreak of roundworm infestation in puppies in a kennel the variation in the extent of the infection is probably almost entirely of environmental origin, including proximity to the infection, frequency of medication, etc. Thus we could say that the heritability of roundworm infection was nought per cent.

Hip dysplasia is a well-known and common abnormality in a number of breeds and it illustrates many genetic principles which have been explained so far. The important issues appear to be:
1 Is hip dysplasia a genetic disorder?
2 Why is the disorder so common in so many breeds?
3 Why, when two X-rayed clear dogs are mated can affected offspring be produced?

Let's take these questions in turn.

1 Hip dysplasia is clearly in part genetic. Neither a dominant nor a recessive mode of transmission fits the available data. Various authors have proposed models of single genes, either dominant or recessive with varying or incomplete penetrance and expressivity. The terms 'penetrance' and 'expressivity' are simply admissions that the genetic control of a particular character is not fully understood. A more realistic approach is to accept that the expression of many genes depends on both the genetic and the non-genetic environment. A polygenic model does fit, and the disorder is quantitative in expression with a range in hip status from perfect to severely dysplastic. The heritability has been estimated to be in the range 25 to 40 per cent. The environmental influences are considerable in amount but much disputed in type and probably include interactions between early growth rate, nutrition and exercise.

2 There are a number of possible genetic contributions to the high frequency of hip dysplasia. One is that in the development of a breed the combination of genes which has gradually been selected because it results in some desirable skeletal shape, is also the formula predisposing to hip weakness. Another is that a gene which has a desirable effect on some aspect of the breed standard could be physically very close on a chromosome to a gene which is undesirable regarding hips. So, unless there is an exchange of chromosomal material as described on page 25, you cannot have one without the other. Additionally, it is perhaps significant that hip dysplasia is found most often in some of the larger breeds, which suggests that size itself and its associated mechanical stresses could also be contributory factors.

3 Because hip dysplasia has a heritability of between 25 and 40 per cent this means that the phenotype of an animal, in this context its X-rayed hip status, does not necessarily reflect its genotype. Let us suggest that three genes, a, b and c (each with alternative alleles + for better hips and — for worse hips) are involved in the variation in hip status. And let us say that in an optimal environment for development three or more + alleles result in perfect hips, but five + alleles are needed in a less than optimal environment. Then the genotypes $a^+a^-b^+b^-c^+c^-$ and $a^+a^+b^+b^-c^+c^+$ could both have perfect hips.

However if we were to mate these two and the gametes happened to be $a^-b^-c^-$ and $a^+b^-c^+$ respectively, then the resulting offspring would have only two + alleles (his genotype would be $a^+a^-b^-b^-c^+c^-$) and could well develop hip dysplasia. So the genetic contribution to hip status can only really be ascertained by breeding records. It is very important to use for breeding only those animals with the best hips because although there will be occasional disappointment, gradually we will change the average genotype towards more + and less — alleles, and therefore decrease the incidence of hip dysplasia. I do hope that this rather detailed examination of the joint contribution of genotype and environment to the variation in quantitative characters has made clear this most important part of genetics.

Choice of Breeding System

We now reach the logical conclusion of the theory explained in this chapter, but it is quite amazing that having fully understood the theory some breeders will still totally disregard it in their breeding plans. The breeding of pedigree dogs for the show ring and for working are similar in their objective, ie improvement of the breed, but the improvement desired involves almost exclusively looks in the former (cosmetic breeds) and function in the latter (functional breeds). Alongside general improvement in all breeds is the attempt to eradicate inherited abnormality, of which there are two types distinguished by their casual origin.

The first is typified by such conditions as PRA, hereditary cataract and quadriplegia. These are due to autosomal recessive genes which have arisen by mutation at some time during the development of the breed. They are thus unfortunate chance occurrences and, hopefully, will gradually be reduced in frequency by properly organised selective breeding.

The other type of inherited abnormality is a direct result of selection for some form of structural extreme: entropion associated with tiny eyes, dermatitis in breeds developed with excessive skin folds and respiratory problems in brachycephalic breeds. These problems are confined to cosmetic breeds and would soon disappear if the breed standards were redesigned with functional normality in mind.

As a result of the different emphasis which is apparent in breeding the diversity of pedigree dogs, two breeding systems are used, inbreeding and outbreeding, and each will now be described.

INBREEDING

Inbreeding is a breeding system where the relationship between the individual mated pairs is closer than the average relationships within the breed. For practical purposes, this means mating a pair with one or more common ancestors in the previous three generations. Thus a second-cousin mating would be a relatively mild form of inbreeding, but brother/sister or parent/offspring mating would both be severe forms of inbreeding. The result of inbreeding is simply to make animals homozygous for a proportion of their genes, and the closer the inbreeding, and the more generations it is continued, the more homozygous and identical the animals become. Is this good or bad?

Well, it depends what is required. It is interesting to note in passing that all wild animal populations which have been investigated have been found to be highly heterozygous (ie a large proportion of the genes are heterozygous for variant alleles). Another fact is that experimental inbreeding in laboratory and farm animals has shown that levels of inbreeding which are commonly exceeded in dog breeding result in significant decreases in fertility, litter size, milk yield of dams, body size, general fitness and disease resistance. There are also reports that inbreeding increases aggression and other antisocial behaviour.

Inbreeding does, however, lead to genetic uniformity and this principle has been extensively used in the production of totally homozygous – and therefore genotypically identical – strains of laboratory mice and rats. But, in the course of inbreeding both favourable and unfavourable recessive alleles will become homozygous and will therefore be expressed. Where these result in abnormalities, losses will occur. The production of highly inbred strains of laboratory rodents has involved losses which just could not be tolerated in most dog breeds without their total extinction.

Dominant alleles will of course also become homozygous and individuals who are homozygous for a dominant allele can be guaranteed to transmit the characteristic to all their offspring. Breeders can often make a distinction between those animals which have this ability to stamp their own desirable characteristics on their offspring and those which are rather less predictable. The former, often rather unscientifically referred to as being prepotent, are probably homozygous for some desired dominant alleles, whereas the latter are more likely to be heterozygous, or even homozygous for the recessive variants.

Two types of breeding, which result in different degrees of inbreeding, are common in pedigree dogs. One is the mating of like to like, ie mating based on phenotypic resemblance, and the other is line breeding. Because most aspects of looks are to some extent heritable, then mating like to like inevitably means that the mated pairs have a genotypic resemblance. Thus a degree of homozygosity results, but this is relatively slight and only significant for characteristics of high heritability. Line breeding is rather more specific. It is a means of increasing the genetic contribution of a particular individual in a line and is planned with direct reference to the pedigree. Each time a stud is needed, the favoured male or one of his close descendents is used and the resulting degree of homozygosity depends on the closeness of the relationship of the mated pairs. The aim of line breeding is that each line should be 'trade marked' by the particular features of one dog; but, because this means an increase in homozygosity the problems of inbreeding already described cannot be avoided.

OUTBREEDING

Outbreeding is the opposite of inbreeding and is therefore the mating of pairs of individuals whose relationship is more distant than the average relationship within the breed (no common ancestors within the previous three generations). Also, its results – maximising heterozygosity, and consequences, variety and non-uniformity – are opposite to those of inbreeding. We can argue that this is both bad and good in the same way that inbreeding was discussed. Clearly any rare unfavourable recessives remain hidden in the heterozygous state, and therefore pose no problems. Outbred animals tend to be bigger and better in terms of vigour and fitness, and also perhaps less aggressive than their inbred counterparts. For this reason functional breeds, or sections of breeds, such as racing Greyhounds and Whippets, Labradors and German Shepherds trained as guide dogs as well as the various gun and sheep dog breeds, are outbred rather than inbred. Not surprisingly these dogs suffer fewer rare recessive abnormalities and disorders of multifactorial origin than the cosmetic breeds, probably as a direct result of their greater heterozygosity.

In summary, therefore, it is up to the breeders to plan their breeding programme to make intelligent use of a combination of the best features offered by inbreeding and outbreeding.

3 Pedigree and Parentage

When you begin breeding the wisest course is to follow the old maxim 'mate the best to the best and hope for the best'. However, with some understanding of genetics and a knowledge of your own breed you can gain a great deal by the careful study of pedigrees. Added to this, your bitch might not be the best – few of us can afford to purchase the best at maturity even supposing a breeder was willing to sell. There is also the little matter of luck! Naturally, we try to minimise chance as far as possible but there is always an element of fortune in any mating.

To begin at the beginning: every adult dog is the combination of two specialist cells which united and became one. However, the genetic material which is contained in each of the original cells is not simply a product of the individual from which it comes. The attributes of its immediate predecessor will therefore not necessarily appear in the progeny. You will hear from many breeders that such and such a bitch is 'the image of her granddam' and in these passing words is contained a great truth, which is that the *family* of a particular dog or bitch is, in general, more important than the individual. Naturally, we would all, ideally, like to use the best dog or bitch we can afford but it is important to remember that poor stock can occasionally produce a flier, and his or her progeny are much more likely to take after the many mediocre animals in the family than the one that showed excellence.

Each animal (humans included) makes a contribution to the gene pool as one generation succeeds another and each individual is one manifestation of the gene pool. The more uniform the pool is between two mated cells the closer the offspring will resemble the parents. If the pools are not so similar the offspring will tend to resemble one parent more than the other in some respects and the other parent in others.

What all this means in practice is that a mediocre dog and bitch both from families of high-quality dogs are much more likely to produce puppies of good quality than a pair that are good themselves but are the product of poor strains. It also means that one good parent from a good strain is likely to stamp their type on a litter so that you might well obtain some quite good puppies from a rather average bitch if you choose the stud dog carefully. We call this ability 'prepotence' (although, as explained in the previous chapter, this is not a strictly accurate term and we should really use the scientifically acceptable 'homozygosity') and to estimate the degree of prepotence in a particular dog we must look at his progeny from several different matings.

This is where your knowledge and 'eye' for your own breed and your own breeding become so important. It is no easy matter to assess quality in a particular dog and even more difficult to assess potential. Furthermore, these generalisations are no more than that; because something is 'likely' or 'probable' does not mean that it will necessarily occur. The whole process of reproduction is complicated beyond our understanding and, although the research of geneticists has enabled us to make educated guesses, knowledge and experience – much of which becomes almost instinctive over the years – are essential factors in successful long-term breeding. It is this experience and understanding that enable our top breeders to maintain their high standards, and it is the lack of such experience which contributes to those early litters which cannot be described as successful.

This six-week-old Norfolk Terrier puppy has found an unusual plaything

SIRE	G. PARENTS	G.G. PARENTS	G.G.G. PARENTS
Cullabine Reppo	Ch. Cullabine Fredrik	Ch. Cullabine Tophunter Turre	Finnish Ch. Pete
			Finnish Ch. Nasse
		Ch. Cullabine Kiho Tipsa	Finnish Ch. Lukko
			Kiho Taju
	Ch. Cullabine Lakka	Ch. Cullabine Tophunter Turre	Finnish Ch. Pete
			Finnish Ch. Nasse
		Ch. Cullabine Nassa	Cullabine Tophunter Tommi
			Ch. Cullabine Una of Snowland

DAM			
Ch. Toveri Tippi	Cullabine Robin	Ch. Cullabine Bobi	Cullabine Tophunter Tommi
			Ch. Cullabine Kiho Tipsa
		Cullabine Zita	Ch. Cullabine Tophunter Turre
			Ch. Cullabine Nassa
	Ch. Cullabine Greta	Ch. Cullabine Aureole	Cullabine Tophunter Tommi
			Ch. Cullabine Una of Snowland
		Cullabine Cleo	Cullabine Tophunter Tommi
			Ch. Cullabine Kiho Tipsa

Pedigree of the bitch Toveri Tassi. Born 22 November 1977. Bred by the author

The pedigree above and your own research can tell you a lot. Toveri Tassi is one of the best bitches I have bred so her pedigree is worthy of considerable study. I bred her mother, who was the youngest-ever bitch Champion in the breed, from Cullabine stock and she was closely line-bred from just five great-great-grandparents. The closest line-breeding would have been to Bobi or Aureole, but I did not think that I wanted to line-breed that closely. I wanted to retain the best elements of Tippi's line but bring in other desirable characteristics from Cullabine stock. (Had I used Robin or a brother or son to Tippi I would have been inbreeding.)

As Tommi features prominently in Tippi's pedigree, I decided that I wanted a dog descended from a close relative so I looked for successful progeny of his brother, Turre. (Both Tommi and Turre were whelped in quarantine out of a bitch imported from Finland.) The dog I chose, Cullabine Reppo, has seldom been shown but he was exactly the type Tippi seemed to need. He had sired one other litter and I was able to see two of the puppies. The bitch to whom Reppo had been mated was also studied. She was quite unrelated and not so closely line-bred as Reppo so it was difficult to estimate the degree of prepotency, but it seemed worth a try as her puppies had been of very good quality.

The resulting litter was excellent and, in fact, Reppo has since been used on another of my bitches just as successfully. Since 1977 I have felt that a further and more fundamental outcross was necessary so I imported a bitch from Finland which is a descendant of Finnish Ch. Pete. I am now engaged in combining the two lines.

This Chow Chow puppy at twelve weeks old really looks as if he is enjoying life

The Bitch

The saying that a kennel is founded on its bitches may be a bit hackneyed but it is none the less very true. The reasons are not hard to find, the most important being that each bitch can only produce a certain number of puppies in her lifetime so that the number of her offspring that can be observed is far fewer than that of a well-used stud dog. As her potential can therefore be less easily assessed it is that much more important to leave less to chance and breed from the best bitch from the best family that you can possibly afford. As we have seen, this is not absolutely essential but the higher up the ladder you begin the better your chances of reaching the top! Of course, you may not be particularly interested in quality in your puppies. If you have a bitch which is the family pet you may well only require a companion or replacement, but if your interest is now, or is likely to be, breeding or showing then the quality of your bitch (and her family, of course) are of the utmost importance. The following, how-ever, applies to any bitch which is being considered for mating.

Your bitch must be lean, strong and in excellent physical condition. She must have an impeccable temperament and should be between one-year and three-and-a-half years old. If you have any knowledge of the background of your bitch she should pre-ferably have come from a line which is known to be fertile and which whelps easily. Her physical condition is of prime importance. An overweight bitch, already carrying around much more than she needs, will find the extra weight of puppies and fluids tiring before she ever gets to the strain of whelping. However, just being thin is not right either. All her muscles should be hard and strong; when she comes to whelp every one will be called upon to help in the delivery of the pups and any slackness will make her task far more difficult. Naturally, she must be sound to start with and of good conformation. It is often said that a slightly oversize bitch is more suitable for breeding, but I have not found this to be true. Neither is it true that a bitch with a long loin has more room for the development of all the puppies conceived. A number of breed standards suggest this is so but the idea is totally fallacious. The most important thing is that everything should fit together. There should be no trace of awkwardness in her stance or her movement and she should have that indefinable bounce of good health.

FEEDING

Your bitch should be fed a mixed diet consisting of meat (lean meat, fat and offal), biscuit, table scraps (including vegetables) and the occasional drop of milk or egg (although egg white must *always* be cooked). I have found it best to avoid uncooked pork – but that's about all! Given a varied diet such as this she should not need any extras. However, if you feel happier giving her a vitamin supplement as part of her normal diet it will do no harm so long as you do not give too much – but it is unlikely to do any more for her either. There is some prejudice among breeders against tinned or dried all-in-one foods, but my own view is that so long as you feed a well-known make your animals will be perfectly healthy. Many of the big manufacturers are pri-marily concerned with feed for farm animals and a tremendous amount of research has gone into the subject of diet from which the world of dogs has benefited. So there is no reason to suppose that such feeds are not nourishing and safe. Personally, I feed a mixed diet – but only because I feel it is probably more interesting for the dogs.

Whatever you feed, do keep a careful eye on your bitch. Some breeds carry more weight than others quite naturally but I still like to be able to feel each individual rib beneath the coat and see a spring in the step. If you watch her trot off the lead she should move smoothly and freely, any tendency to clumsiness and you should begin to wonder if you are not giving her too much to eat. Incidentally, as with humans, there is no necessity for sugar in the diet!

EXERCISE

Exercise is also necessary to keep your bitch in peak condition. Regular walks both on and off the lead are essential, however much of a chore you feel it to be. My experience has been that the most active and energetic dogs are the best whelpers and the ones who would prefer to stay indoors are the ones that present you with problems. If you have more than one dog and a reasonable sized garden this can help a lot. The best sort of garden is one with a long side that overlooks something interesting as this will keep them busy running up and down most of the time!

TEMPERAMENT

The question of temperament is one to which much thought should be given. It is inexcusable to mate a bitch to 'improve' her; if your bitch is too fine in bone or 'shelly' it is unlikely that she will 'body up' as the result of having a litter. The same applies if she is highly-strung, nervous or shy – having puppies might easily make her positively aggressive so she is best left unserved. You also hear people say that every bitch 'ought' to have a litter. Although it is true that a maiden bitch is more likely to develop pyometra, the likelihood of her getting it is slight in any case. The likelihood of there being a complication during pregnancy, whelping or suckling is much greater!

A good brood bitch must be friendly, stable and bold. She can be a good guard dog without being aggressive and she can be cautious of strangers without being shy. Experience shows that the family pet finds the transition to motherhood more difficult than those bitches who are less cosseted. The family pet is often very concerned about her little comforts which she has come to expect, and occasionally resents the discomfort occasioned by carrying pups. This does not normally result in neglect of puppies once they are born, but if their temperament is not really stable some bitches may well show signs of distress during pregnancy which could affect their trustworthiness.

Similar problems can arise if a bitch is mated too young as she may think of her litter as toys to be played with rather than puppies to be looked after but, in any case, it is not really fair to mate a bitch until she is fully mature. With some of the larger breeds this might be over two years old but most bitches are ready by their second season or at around eighteen months old. I do not believe that it is necessary to mate young while the bone of the pelvis is still 'green' but I do think that every bitch gets to an age where the strain of a first litter might be too much for her. I would talk to your veterinary surgeon if you are considering mating a bitch for the first time which is over four years old.

CONDITION

Finally, you should keep the bitch in peak condition at all times. Apart from the above, she should be regularly wormed, her skin and her ears and teeth should be examined regularly and any problems dealt with immediately. She should always be kept up-to-date with her booster vaccinations and if one is due during her pregnancy this should be brought forward to a couple of months before her season is due. You should also consult your vet if your bitch has had any serious illness (which might have affected heart, liver or kidneys) or has ever slipped a disc or had a broken limb.

The above applies to all bitches whether they are crossbred or pedigree.

Hereditary Defects

If you are breeding from pedigree stock, whether dog or bitch, you have some further points to consider. First and foremost is the question of hereditary defects. These are all the result of combinations of genes which lead to a weakness rather than a strength. Some conditions are so interdependent (polygenic) that their complexities may never be unravelled, while others are the result of a fairly straightforward recessive factor which may be overcome given sufficient time and determination. An example of the former is the difficult and thorny question of hip dysplasia which was once thought to have been the result of breeding for a longer, sloping backline and an increased turn of stifle, ie a simple weakness due to a long-term and deliberate change of conformation. If you look at any pictures of pre- and just post-war German Shepherds you will see exactly what I mean. However, the condition has now become apparent in many breeds, some of which have not suffered such a change of conformation. So many factors are involved, some of which are not essentially genetic but have to do with feeding, weight gain compared to size and strength of bone in growing puppies and exercise.

An example of the simple recessive type is Progressive Retinal Atrophy, known as PRA. This is gradual blindness resulting from a combination of recessive genes which can be eliminated by not using stock which carries the recessive gene. Actually it sounds simpler than it is, but elimination is possible. There are other conditions between these two extremes, including entropion and cryptorchidism, and related problems are the back problems encountered in some of the long-backed breeds and the eye and breathing problems related to the brachycephalic breeds. I do not intend to deal with these defects in any depth, they are included to help illustrate the various pitfalls which lie in the path of the prospective breeder.

It is absolutely essential that you learn as much about your own breed as you possibly can and that you select the stud dog you use with care. Some of the hereditary defects are the subject of special provisions of the Kennel Club. In conjunction with their veterinary advisors, the Kennel Club administers schemes whereby breeders can have their brood bitches and stud dogs tested under controlled conditions. A certificate of freedom from the condition is issued if the tests have proved satisfactory.

Schemes are currently operated for hereditary cataract, PRA and hip dysplasia. The Kennel Club has also formed a sub-committee to study hip dysplasia, eye problems in general, cryptorchidism, luxating patella (dislocation of the knee joint) and jaw and teeth structure. The committee expects to study elongated soft palates (a condition sometimes found in some of the short-faced breeds), epilepsy, hernias, pyloric stenosis (narrow stomach exit which prevents proper digestion of food) and a number of muscular conditions, at a later stage.

Family Planning

Line breeding, inbreeding and outcrossing have already been discussed in Dr Pidduck's chapter on genetics and now we come to the practical applications of this information. The owner of the bitch has a distinct advantage over the owner of the stud dog: a bitch can be mated to any one of a wide spectrum of dogs. By studying the pedigree of your bitch you can see exactly what stage of breeding has been reached and you can move closer to the line or further from it as you think best. As you come to a decision try to keep a balance between the knowledge you have of both pedigrees on paper and the families and progeny of the dog that you have seen. This is easy to say but not so easy to do. We see a magnificent dog in the ring, especially one that has done a great deal of winning, and without really thinking things out we make a sub-conscious judgment that this is exactly the dog we need. We may be right but, as

Tibetan Spaniels at six weeks old. They are not likely to stay in that basket for long

many have found to their cost, unless the gene pools fit together a litter of quite ordinary puppies can be the result. So trace the pedigrees back, see as many dogs in the pedigree as you can, see as many of the dog's progeny as you can and keep a note-book or scrapbook with the comments of experienced breeders and photographs, where possible, of dogs of the past. You will make the best use of your bitch by under-standing the basic principles of heredity outlined in the previous chapter and by gathering together as much information as possible about the dogs and bitches (particularly the prepotent ones) and strains within your breed.

One further thing: making up a champion in Britain is probably more difficult than in any other country in the world and it is for this reason that we maintain our place as the most consistent supplier of top-quality stock to other breeders in every corner of the globe. However, this does not mean that it is impossible to make up dogs which are not of the highest quality or, on the other hand, that the best dogs will necessarily become champions. One of the dogs in my own lines has hardly ever been shown but at one stage I needed an outcross and from his pedigree and family details he fitted the bill exactly. I was lucky and right − however hard you work and however much care you take luck still plays a part.

If you intend to breed seriously it is likely that you will quickly invest in another bitch. Just as much care should be taken in adding to your stock as with your original purchase. You need a bitch which is of similar, but preferably not identical, breeding and one which has the good points lacking in your foundation bitch. The time may come when you feel ready to keep a stud dog and it is probably the combination of these two bitches over several generations which will result in that consistent Best of Breed winner and the successful prepotent stud.

If you own three or more bitches which you use for breeding you will need a breeder's licence from your local council. They will charge a 'realistic fee' related to the cost of issuing the licence. Your premises will be inspected by a representative of the local authority to ensure that they are suitable before the licence is granted. The legislation requiring these licences was enacted in 1973, the idea being to restrict the breeding of puppies to approved premises. In fact, as predicted at the time by those with real knowledge and understanding of the problems, the act has entirely failed to cope with the real abuses, ie the activities of the trading kennels which buy in numerous very young puppies for resale.

The Dog

Few people suddenly decide that they want to breed dogs and start looking round for a suitable bitch. The idea that it might be interesting, enjoyable and, just possibly, profitable takes root only slowly, and then usually after some experience of owning or showing a dog. Unfortunately, if you already own a dog rather than a bitch your activities are rather restricted. Firstly, the owners of bitches usually have a wide choice of stud dogs and, unless you are very lucky and your dog is absolutely out-standing, most breeders will go to a stud dog owner who can offer them a choice of dog and can also show some evidence that their stock produces progeny of quality. Most breeders, too, prefer to go to someone who has experience in mating dogs of

their breed and on whom they can rely for advice regarding their choice. Another difficulty is that your dog has, in all probability, been brought up as a member of the
family and whenever he has shown signs of mating behaviour will have been sharply
told that such displays are not acceptable. By the time a dog is two-and-a-half years old
this training might easily prevent him from ever mating a bitch.

If you want to breed and you have a good dog − get a good bitch to go with him and
start from scratch. However, do not automatically assume that they should be mated.
You should still regard your own dog as one of a number who might be suitable and be
just as careful in your selection as if you did not have a dog of your own. More
disappointing litters have been bred simply because the dog and the bitch were there
than for any other reason!

There are problems in keeping a dog and a bitch together in the average household,
of course, but these can be overcome with time, patience, potions and pills. Any dog
in close proximity to a bitch in-season for any length of time without being allowed to
mate is likely to complain and howl at best and lose weight and condition at worst. I
believe that it is essential to make arrangements to keep them completely apart during
the time of the bitch's season, either in a separate part of your house and garden or by
putting the dog into kennels for a short period. As well as keeping them well away
from each other your bitch should be well dosed with Amplex or Anti-mate (do not
bother with the various proprietary sprays − most of the stud dogs I know completely ignore them!). This will mask the scent in her vaginal discharge and in her
urine, although it is unlikely to be totally effective. An alternative is to use the
contraceptive pill. A great deal of work has been done by pharmacologists to develop a
wide safety margin and they have carried out exhaustive tests to ensure that there are
no side effects from these drugs. They can be used to suppress the heat entirely or to
postpone it for periods up to six months. The basic chemical involved is megestrol
acetate but the correct dosage is absolutely vital so the pills are only available through
your veterinary surgeon.

To sum up: my personal feeling is that if you have both bitches and dogs and you
are serious about breeding you should have proper kennel facilities. It is not impossible to operate without such premises but it is very difficult and, I believe, not really
fair on your stock to 'box and cox' with them all the time.

If you have a dog which you are sure would be in demand as a stud much of the
advice already given regarding bitches should be closely followed. Although general
physical condition is not as essential as it is in a bitch because the dog will not have to
take the strain of bearing the puppies, nevertheless nobody is likely to want to use him
unless he looks good, so make sure that he is always lean and fit. Apart from being an
excellent specimen of the particular breed, he must, of course, be temperamentally
sound. A good guard dog does not have to be aggressive, neither should caution be
confused with shyness. But remember that potential users of his services can only go
on what they see when they are considering the dog, and therefore he should be
friendly, stable and bold with other dogs and with strangers.

If your breed is one in which there are hereditary problems it is important that your
dog should have undergone the relevant tests and have the necessary certificates.

Never be tempted to allow him to be used if there is any question about his hereditary fitness – you will only damage your breed's reputation and your own! It is only right, too, that your dog should be fully vaccinated, regularly wormed and that his skin and coat should be clean and free from infestation or infection. This may appear to be stating the obvious but in the same way that you are entitled to only allow your dog to be mated to bitches that you consider are suitable, the bitch owner is entitled not to use him if he does not look properly cared for. A matted coat, fleas or flea dirt, a mucky dog-run or stained teeth are all evidence of a lack of concern. However good your dog, bitches will not be brought a second time if their owners do not feel that you are taking your responsibilities seriously.

Every owner has their own individual ideas about feeding and the owners of stud dogs are no exception. Additions of yeast, egg, liver or other, more exotic potions are all claimed to be the 'extra' that a stud dog needs. This may be right, although our dogs are all fed a good, mixed and balanced diet and they seem to perform well without any extras!

Full details of kennel records are given towards the end of the book but, in passing, it should be mentioned that records of the litters sired by your dogs are most important. The owner of the bitch sees the puppies constantly during the first few weeks of their life and will certainly follow their careers, especially if they are shown. There can be many more puppies from any one sire so it is more difficult to keep track of them but the effort is well worth while. Also the owners of most bitches will be particularly interested in the progeny of your dog so it is important to be able to give them accurate details and, if possible, show them photographs. The participation of the dog in any litter is brief but both dog and bitch owner share equal responsibility for the quality of the litter and, through each generation, for the future of their breed.

4 Mating

'You can be absolutely sure that there will be no problems at all mating your bitch if you do not want her mated. Any difficulties arise only when you want her to stand for a particular dog and the problems increase in inverse proportion to the distance travelled. The nearer home you are the easier it will be!' This is the rather cynical view of a friend of mine who says that he has the figures to prove his assertion – and I must admit that it does sometimes seem that he must be right. However, I do assure you that the difficulties decrease with experience, although I would be the first to admit that this information is not much comfort when you realise that your bitch has missed.

It is certainly true that some breeds are more difficult to mate than others. Sometimes the problems are physical conformation and sometimes psychological – and, of course, a pet bitch (ie one that has the undivided attention of her family) often does not take kindly to being interfered with. Here, again, knowing your own breed is most important. Most difficulties will eventually be overcome by instinct on the part of the dog and bitch and patience on the part of the owner, although if you have a Chow Chow or Greyhound or one of the other tricky breeds you might well need help to begin with. Fortunately, most stud dog owners are reasonably experienced and can usually be relied upon to be helpful. Be cautious in getting together two maiden dogs and two novice owners – they might be lucky but they are more likely to spend a couple of days messing about to no purpose!

WHERE

The usual practice is to bring the bitch to the dog when she is thought to be ready. The owner of a dog used regularly at stud will have a place, whether it be a room of the house, a kennel run or a garage, where his dog usually works and the dog will be well aware of what is happening almost before he gets the scent of the bitch. At one time, and in America it is still very common practice because of the distances involved, it was usual for the owner of the bitch to put her on the train to the nearest station to the stud dog owner. The bitch would be sent just before she was ready, would be mated (perhaps twice) and then returned the same way. In some ways this made a miss less likely as the bitch could be left a few extra days if she was a little early and no one was inconvenienced. However, it also meant that the owner of the bitch had no real guarantee that she had been mated to the dog requested and it is now much more common for the bitch's owner to personally take the bitch to the dog. Two matings obviously means two journeys and so many owners just have the one service, cross

However concerned and careful you are to provide the very best of whelping boxes in the best of rooms. . .

their fingers and hope for the best.

The Kennel Club has a regulation which forbids the mating of bitches within the precincts of a show – but this does not mean that a mating cannot take place outside the boundary fence and, if convenient, this practice avoids a long extra journey. Owners will also sometimes meet at a place about halfway between their two residences, and many matings have taken place beside a motorway service station car park! To my mind these practices are not satisfactory and I believe matings under these circumstances are less likely to be successful. The business is usually rushed which makes the bitch nervous and tense, the dog is in a strange place and may not perform so readily and the bitch's owner is likely to hope for the best as regards the timing of the mating to fit in with other plans.

The most sensible solution is for the owner of the bitch (having informed the stud dog owner of approximately the time the stud will be required) to take the bitch to the stud dog at the earliest time that the mating is feasible. On arrival the mating can take place so that the bitch's owner can be assured that the dog requested is being used. If the bitch is not quite ready she should be left at the kennels until she has been mated. At this stage the stud dog owner can contact the bitch's owner, the bitch can be collected and another mating allowed on arrival. I prefer two matings but, so long as the bitch will readily accept the dog, there is no necessity for this. Statistically there is an increased conception rate if there are two matings at a forty-eight hour interval. Of my last two litters one bitch was mated three times and another was mated once. They both had five puppies – a slightly larger than average litter in my breed.

THE BITCH

A bitch will usually come into season at between five and eleven months old. The smaller breeds tend to mature earlier than the average (about seven months) and the larger ones later. Thereafter she will come into season at regular intervals of about six months. Again, there is no specific pattern but most bitches remain regular once their own pattern has been established (unless it has been upset by a litter or false pregnancy). I have bitches by which you could set a six-month calendar, others which vary by as much as two months from season to season and one which comes in regularly at nine-month intervals. There is also a number of breeds, Basenjis for example, which only come into season once a year.

The reproductive cycle is: for five to six months after completion of a heat period the whole reproductive system lies dormant; this is the anoestrus period. About ten days before oestrus proper begins the vulva starts to swell (pre-oestrus) and by the time oestrus begins the vulva is greatly enlarged. This is the time to keep a careful eye on her as some dogs are so clean that you could easily miss the first few days. A bitch is usually ready to mate between ten and sixteen days after the first coloured discharge from the vulva and if not mated will return to the next anoestrus period in a further fourteen days. During the time the bitch may conceive the coloured discharge clears.

. . . the attraction of a hole in the garden is difficult to resist

The vulva remains swollen and moist during this period but the colour returns at the end of the acceptance stage. Occasionally bitches will have a colourless season. If they are served when the vulva is at its maximum enlargement and she is prepared to stand for the dog she will often conceive.

Even if not mated the bitch may show signs of being in-whelp, she may put on weight and, after six to eight weeks, begin to scrabble about and dig and even produce milk. This is known as a 'false' (if she has not been mated) or 'phantom' pregnancy (if she has been mated but has not conceived) although there is no clinical difference. I have found it best to be rather less than sympathetic with any of my bitches when they develop a false pregnancy. More and longer walks, regular disturbance when they are settled and plenty of 'rough and tumble' games seem to be the most effective cure. Love, sympathy and understanding only seem to make them more maternal and certainly prolong the symptoms. If you have a bitch who really frets and has swollen teats, a consultation with your veterinary surgeon is probably best. There are a number of drugs which will quickly alleviate the symptoms and dry up the milk flow.

Another problem to look out for at this stage, especially in a bitch which has never been mated and more particularly if a bitch has been mated but has had a false pregnancy, is the condition known at pyometra. This is an infection of the uterus which can become so enlarged that the swelling is clearly visible. The bitch will go off her food, drink a great deal and be generally off colour about eight or nine weeks after the season. Pyometra may be either 'open' or 'closed', the open type resulting in a considerable discharge from the vulva. In either case you should consult your veterinary surgeon immediately and his likely advice is that the bitch should have an immediate operation to remove the uterus. The presence of pus does make such an operation dangerous so it is more sensible to have a pet bitch spayed if she is particularly subject to false pregnancies.

THE DOG

The way in which you treat your prospective stud dog during his formative months can make or mar him. He must have confidence in himself and confidence in you so get him used to being handled but never check him for sexual play. This is sometimes difficult if your dogs live as members of the family but you will have to put up with the difficulties if he is going to be successful in the future. To be honest, dogs which are intended for use at stud are better kennelled although that does not mean that they should not have plenty of company, both human and canine, and be used to coming into the house regularly. Unfortunately, dogs used at stud often forget any house training that they have been subjected to but you cannot afford to scold them for this.

It is important that your dog is quite used to meeting strangers, both canine and human, on his own ground as well as outside his territory. You will have to be rather protective towards him, though, whenever he comes into contact with other dogs and bitches; his young curiosity must inevitably lead him to sniff at other dogs enthusiastically and an older dog or bitch may not welcome the attention and snap at him. This could also make him very wary when the time comes for him to be confident and willing. Most young dogs go through an adolescent stage during which their sexual urge is very strong. This is the time when they might go off their food if there are in-season bitches about and they can rapidly lose condition. The phase is short-lived, however, and is replaced by a normal sex drive by about eight months. Most dogs may be used for the first time between eight and eleven months although with the really large breeds which mature much more slowly this can easily be left until eighteen months.

From the time a dog is mature he will be regularly producing semen, some of which, under normal circumstances, is excreted during urination. The idea that the first time a dog is used at stud the fluid contains no semen is quite wrong, but it is usual for a first-time stud not to have a fee until his fertility is 'proved'. Two other points to remember: it is sensible to get the smaller breeds used to being handled on a table and also to get any dog used to being handled when he indulges in sex play. The reasons are simply that it is a good deal more convenient for you if you do not have to kneel down for any length of time and that some bitches are very reticent, even when they are quite ready, and might well need to be held firmly while the dog mounts. A dog that mates 'naturally' may sound all right but a bitch owner who has travelled many miles will expect a competent performance − and you can be sure that the stud dog will be held responsible if he will not mate the bitch. In any case, it is much more satisfactory to have a simple, controlled mating; allowing both dog and bitch to run about all over the place can easily damage the dog if anything goes wrong during the turn.

It is a good idea to have a length of three-inch bandage handy in the place you use for mating bitches. If the bitch is upset you can then quickly make a comfortable muzzle for her. You simply pass the bandage round the mouth, crossing it over under the jaw, and then tie off the two long ends behind the skull. Such a muzzle is not designed to protect you or the bitch's owner (although it certainly can) but to protect the dog!

The first time your dog is used at stud it is sensible to use one of your own experienced bitches. This is because you will need plenty of time and patience if you are to achieve the desired result and, particularly if you are not experienced, you do not then have an anxious owner sitting waiting in your kitchen or, worse still, looking over your shoulder and offering advice! Unlimited patience is absolutely essential. You must not worry your dog and, although it is usually possible to get a satisfactory service it does sometimes take a considerable time.

The bigger breeds sometimes have less sex drive so if you are the proud owner of an Irish Wolfhound or a Great Dane you may need to give them some extra help. A wide length of material which can go round the stomach will help support and restrain the bitch and will also ensure that the dog does not have to lift her as well as find the right place!

WHEN

The owner of the stud dog should be informed that you wish to use the dog at the time the bitch comes into season. You both know that it will probably be within the following three weeks, but it is tempting fate to make definite arrangements. The time when a bitch is ready to stand not only varies from dog to dog but from season to season so a bitch that was mated on her ninth day at her first service might not be ready until her sixteenth day the second time around. I have had bitches not ready until the twenty-fourth day and a friend has a bitch that was mated and conceived a full litter on the twenty-ninth day!

As soon as you notice the colour examine the bitch every day, testing the discharge with a piece of white kitchen roll or cottonwool. You will probably find that as you take the test she tries to sit down, but sometime after the ninth day she will stay standing while you wipe the vulva. A day or two after she will 'flick' her tail. This is a difficult movement to visualise but you will know it when you see it; the tail takes on a life of its own and twists at right angles to the spine as you touch the vulva. She may now be ready but a further test should confirm it. Thoroughly wash your hands (or use a plastic, disposable surgical glove) and gently insert your middle finger into the bitch's vulva and vagina. The direction is almost vertical, up towards the spine. If the passage is dry use a little KY jelly, but dryness usually means she is not quite ready. Your finger should slide in quite easily, and if you hold it there for a few seconds you should begin to feel the ring of muscles on the inner edge of the vulva contract and pull. If she will do it to you she will do it to the dog so make tracks for the stud dog straight away. If your bitch is a maiden you may well feel a taut cord membrane stretching across the vagina. Ease your finger around this and pull very gently. It should break quite easily but, if it does not, take her along to your veterinary surgeon. Despite being ready your bitch may well be rather tight and, if this is the case, just work your finger around the passage until you feel it become more supple. In fact, an experienced stud dog will not take a blind bit of notice of such an obstruction but it may well put off an inexperienced dog and can be quite painful for the bitch, so it is good for both of them if these simple precautions are observed.

Despite all this you may still be wrong, although my experience is that one tends to be too soon rather than too late, if that is any comfort. The acid test, of course, is the one carried out by the dog. An experienced dog will not normally bother with a bitch unless she is quite ready and will certainly not waste any time if she is.

When the dog and the bitch are brought together allow them to play together for a few minutes – assuming the bitch is prepared to be friendly! The dog may be very keen and start to mount but, without upsetting him, try to avoid this – partly for the reasons for holding the bitch given above but mainly because if he gets too excited too soon he might well mount and miss and the most valuable fraction of his semen could end up on the floor! A young, inexperienced stud dog will tend to get into a muddle and try to mate the bitch from the wrong end or try to work at one of the legs. If you can possibly mate a novice dog to an experienced bitch this can be a great help. She will soon move round to the right position without any help from you.

When you think that both dog and bitch are quite ready the bitch should be held firmly by the collar. An assistant is invaluable during a mating and if you can find someone who is ready to help regularly this is better still. An experienced team can be a great asset as both the dog and the bitch will sense their experience and will work without distraction. With the bitch held still, bring the dog round to the right posi-

Initial inspection

All systems go

tion and place your hand under the bitch's tummy, just behind the vulva. A little pressure here can move the vulva upwards slightly, making entry for the dog that much easier. Apart from gently restraining the dog by the collar let him do his own work. If you try to force him forward he will almost certainly back away. As the dog mounts, the hard, pointed end of his penis should just touch the soft ring of the vulva and at this stage he will drive forward and you should feel the penis slide into the vagina with the hand which is against the bitch's tummy. Letting go of the dog's collar, now press the palm of the hand against the dog's rump and hold him gently in this position for about thirty seconds or so. What happens is that at the base of the dog's penis is a thick ring of engorged tissue like a doughnut. Once the dog has driven into the bitch this ring swells inside the ring of muscle just inside the mouth of the vulva. This sets up a contraction in that ring of muscle which tightens on the base of the penis preventing the blood escaping back into the mainstream of the dog. Until that muscle slackens the dog cannot escape from the bitch and it is this period which is called the 'tie'.

Once the tie has begun you can relax and, very gently, allow the dog to turn. It would be a considerable strain on the dog to maintain the mounted position so he will want to turn quite naturally. When he is ready carefully lift his front legs to the side of the bitch and then one of the back legs over the bitch's back. They will remain in this turned position for anything up to half an hour; generally, a bit less than this, although it can be longer. During this period the third fraction (see the next chapter for full details of the composition of the dog's semen) is ejaculated into the vagina.

Made it!

The tie does not look very comfortable but neither dog nor bitch seems to mind

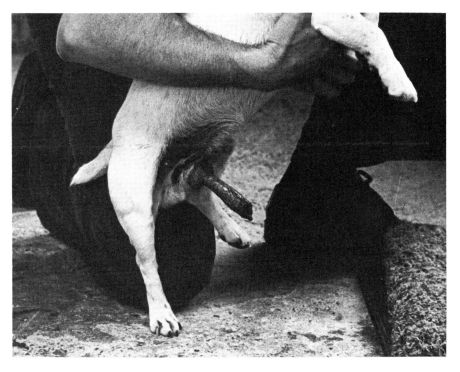

The ring of muscles just inside the vulva grip the swollen base of the penis. The penis cannot subside until the muscles of the vulva relax so the length of the tie is dependent on the bitch, not the dog

Most breeders like to see a good tie but there is no reason why the bitch should not have puppies without a proper tie. The sperm which fertilizes the ova is ejaculated at the beginning of the service and, although it has a great distance to travel and the third fraction will sweep it along, there is no reason why enough sperm should not make the journey on its own.

During the tie both handlers should keep hold of the dogs; they will get bored after quite a short time and may try to pull apart, which can be most painful and their reaction to the pain might be to struggle which could cause damage to both the dog and bitch. So keep them calm and close together until, quite naturally, they come apart. The dog can then be put back into a run − with a word of praise for a job well done − and the bitch returned to her owner. There is no need to carry her, or lay her on her back, or any of the other traditional methods used to ensure that she does not lose any of that valuable sperm. If she had got out and been mated by your local Romeo she would have run all the way home and had a litter of puppies with no help from you at all!

With the bigger and heavier breeds it is as well to have a third person standing by to help during the mating. The bitch may need support when the dog mounts her and the dog may need to be restrained if he is proceeding too enthusiastically in the wrong direction. When they are tied you may also find that the weight of the dog is too much for the bitch so putting the wide band of material round her tummy will enable two people to support her comfortably.

An only bitch that has been kept as a house pet can be very sensitive to her owner and her owner is likely to be over-anxious too. In this case I think it is better to mate the dog and bitch without the owner being there and to let them see the tie when it is all over.

Most matings are fairly straightforward once the dog has had a few bitches. The most common problem I have come across is that of the relative heights of the dog and the bitch. Two average specimens of the breed will obviously be in the right positions but a smallish dog mated to a largish bitch, or vice versa, can mean that the dog is always trying to work in the wrong place. The answer is *not* a quick foray into the house for a pile of magazines or a couple of telephone directories. It is vital that both dog and bitch feel that they are on firm ground without anything rocking, slipping, squeaking or sliding. If your dog is going to be used at stud get a thick piece of chipboard or blockboard with pads of wood at each corner. Its size and final thickness depend on your breed, but it should be about 1¼ ins (30 mm) thick for a medium-sized breed, ½ in. (about 12 mm) for small breeds and about 3 ins (75mm) for large breeds. If the board has a smooth surface cover it by sticking on a piece of old carpet. Its area should be about one and a half times the size of the dog in both directions. If the bitch is too short for the dog simply put her on the board, if she is too tall put the dog on the board. You will quickly learn to judge the relative sizes of your dogs that are used at stud and you will find that you get out the board and place it in the right position automatically. You have no idea how much trouble it can save until you have tried it!

Dogs, like humans, have to go through a formal routine before a mating: the playing, the sniffing and the bouncing are all part of this routine. Occasionally a bitch will arrive who, although quite ready, is not interested in the play part and stands stock-still waiting for the dog to get on with it. This can be just as off-putting for the dog as a bitch who growls at him. If this occurs do not force the dog towards the bitch. If she is light enough, pick her up and flick her tail a few times in the dog's face, making her go through the motions of play with the dog. He will not mind a bit that it is you pulling the strings and after a few minutes he will have gone through his routine and will be ready to have a go. With a big or heavy bitch you have to work a bit harder, lifting her up by her front then her back legs until the dogs gets the idea.

Finally, you must make sure that your dog's penis has fully retracted into its sheath. Normally after a tie the penis is enlarged but flaccid and, as it reduces in size it will naturally retract. However, if the dog has withdrawn before the tie he may well have difficulties at this stage. If an edge of the penile shaft has become trapped in a fold of skin you need to gently pull back the sheath to release it so that it can slide back smoothly. In some of the short-legged breeds the penis will sometimes drag on the ground so you may need to bathe it very gently by dropping warm water onto it from a clean sponge or cottonwool. It is most important that no dirt or grit gets trapped as the penis returns to its sheath. Afterwards both dog and bitch will benefit from a drink, a little cooked egg or warm milk and a rest.

One last tip: if all else fails and you are still sure that the bitch is ready, remove the dog for twenty minutes or so and give him a very light meal. For some reason this will very often do the trick – although I am not sure whether it is the meal or the rest that has the desired effect.

TERMS

When the owner of a bitch approaches the stud dog owner with the request to use the dog, the owner of the dog can accept or refuse the bitch. Most stud dog owners will, rightly, specify 'approved bitches only'. If you have a good stud dog with a sound record of winning progeny you are not likely to allow him to be used on a bitch whose quality is such that the puppies will damage his reputation. However, if the owner does allow the dog to be used then payment for the service will be expected on the day of the mating. As long as a mating has taken place (and this includes a service without a tie) then the fee is payable. Generally, the owner of the stud dog – if it has been proved – will allow a further free mating if the bitch does not have a litter, but they do not have any obligation to do this. If your bitch does not conceive it is only polite to inform the owner of the stud dog as soon as you know. You must not be surprised if you are not allowed a further service if you leave contacting the owner of the stud dog until your bitch next comes into season.

The cost of using a dog at stud varies with the breed and the quality of the dog. At one time the stud fee would be approximately the sale price of one puppy but the economics of breeding puppies have undergone considerable changes in the last twenty years and the price is now about half the sale price of a puppy. However, the fee is entirely in the hands of the stud dog owner and they are entitled to charge whatever they think they can get – the law of supply and demand works here as everywhere else.

If your bitch fails to conceive from two successive matings I would advise a consultation with your veterinary surgeon. Assuming that both matings were successful and that the dog has mated other bitches in the meantime which have conceived, it is only sensible to get professional advice. Do not go around blaming the dog – it is not likely to be his fault. Venereal disease is not common in dogs but it does exist along with plenty of other reasons why a bitch fails to have puppies. These can only be properly diagnosed by your vet.

5 Artificial Insemination
by Dr W. Edward Allen

Despite the fact that the first recorded successful artificial insemination (AI) was carried out in dogs by Spallanzani in 1780, the technique is not commonly employed on Man's best friend at the present time. This early work led to a multimillion-pound industry as far as cattle, and to a lesser extent, pigs are concerned, but very little further work was done using dogs until the 1950s. Since then progress has been made on both the short- and long-term preservation of canine semen, although, at present, conception rates are not as good as those following natural matings.

The Pros and Cons of AI

The reasons for the slow development of AI in dogs are many and varied but they are mainly related to the physiology of the reproductive cycle in the bitch and the way in which Man has chosen to exploit the dog. The situation can be contrasted with that in cattle where the technique of AI has reached a high degree of efficiency and sophistication. In the canine world the demand for any particular sire is limited by the fact that a single mating may result in the production of four to ten offspring, whereas only one, or occasionally two, are produced by cows. Also, bitches which have not conceived will not return to heat for six to nine months but this interval is twenty-one days in cows, so that a cow may have many more attempts to become pregnant than a bitch. It is important to remember that dogs are only required to reproduce in order to transmit (for working or showing etc.) their favourable points. Cattle are required to reproduce at an exaggerated rate in order to provide food for the human population, both in the form of meat (calves) and milk (continued lactation).

To arrange a mating between two particular dogs is relatively simple since dogs are easy to transport (compare this with moving a bull or cow) and because of the fact that a bitch has a pro-oestrus; this means that the mating can be arranged for nine to eleven days after the first signs are obvious, whereas cows are in heat for only fifteen hours and this allows very little time for planning.

In dogs there are relatively few situations in which natural matings cannot take place, and in addition many breeds are so small in number that it would be inadvisable to artificially disseminate the genes of one dog too widely among the population. Furthermore there is a natural prejudice among some people against artificial methods of mating which may be reflected in the attitude of the Kennel Club of Great Britain which will not register the progeny of artificial matings, except in exceptional circumstances. These only include the physical inability to mate and inseminations must be made immediately after collection. The Kennel Club must have agreed to all artificial matings in advance, if puppies are to be registered.

It should always be borne in mind when considering the use of artificial insemination that any mating, whether natural or artificial, is undesirable if one or other of the dogs has a defect which is known to be of an hereditary nature. There are, however, several situations in which AI can usefully be employed, including acquired physical defects such as the loss of a limb and spinal problems.

In my experience, though, the most common problems are those of a psychological nature and probably result from the way in which dogs are treated when young. It is natural for house dogs to practise copulatory movements with household objects around the age of puberty. This behaviour usually does not meet with the approval of householders and is discouraged. Similarly, in situations where many dogs are kept together (e.g. racing kennels) sexual activity invites reprimand. Furthermore, in many situations, e.g. when being walked in the road, encounters between dogs of any sex are either restricted or avoided in case 'unsightly' sniffing behaviour or hostility occur. It is either illegal or antisocial to allow dogs to roam loose due to indiscriminate defaecation, possible damage to property or gardens (especially where there is a bitch in heat) and the possibility of the dog causing a road traffic accident. It is not without good reason that the dog occupies the special position which it does in our society and has come to be called 'Man's best friend', and this ability of the dog to adapt to human values can influence its natural instincts, including those of a sexual nature. These pressures do not usually affect the bitch as severely, although some bitches become so strongly attached to their owners that they will not allow any sort of physical contact with another dog, even when they are in heat.

The results of this restraining human influence is that when dogs are offered the opportunity of copulating naturally they may appear confused or scared. The dog may take no notice of the bitch, may be intimidated by her, or may stand behind the bitch and make copulatory movements without actually mounting. Artificial collection from the dog in this situation on one or more occasions will in many cases stimulate desire and culminate in natural copulation.

Artificial insemination may be useful in situations where it is necessary to avoid direct contact between dogs in order to control the spread of disease. On occasions breeding dogs may contract diseases such as scabies or ringworm; these do not cause ill-health but may be transmitted by direct contact to other animals. There are also two venereal diseases (ie diseases spread by sexual contact) of dogs. One is caused by a bacterium called *brucella canis* and has not been recorded in this country, although some dogs have been shown to have antibodies in their blood to this organism. The second is due to a virus and is called transmissible venereal lymphogranuloma. The condition is seen occasionally in this country, usually as a result of importing dogs from abroad.

In my opinion the more common bacteria which are associated with infertility, e.g. β-haemolytic streptococci (BHS), staphylococci and coliforms etc, are probably not transmitted venereally. These bacteria can be found in the vaginas of many normal bitches, and in the prepuces of dogs. Undoubtedly they can affect fertility if they are introduced into the uterus of some bitches during heat, and treatment to prevent this may be necessary. It will probably be some time before we understand the true relationship between infertility and the presence of bacteria in the reproductive tracts of dogs.

Finally, an established artificial insemination service could increase the number of bitches which a particular dog impregnates, both by disseminating the semen further than it is convenient for the dog to travel and by storing the semen until it is required. Such a service would require strict supervision and is not likely in the foreseeable future.

Normal Copulatory Behaviour

Although the normal copulatory behaviour of dogs is familiar to those involved in dog breeding, it is worth considering at this point the significance of some of the events which occur during the act.

After a variable period of foreplay a normal bitch in oestrus (heat) will allow mounting by the male, at which time the penis is protruded from the sheath. Although the dog's penis is apparently rigid at all times due to the presence of a bone (the *os penis*), at this stage of coitus the *pars longa glandis* is only slightly enlarged, as is the *bulbus glandis*. The dog makes rapid thrusting movements in order to achieve intromission and at the same time ejaculates a small quantity of clear fluid, the first fraction of the ejaculate. Much of this may be voided outside the bitch and although most workers suggest that this fraction originates from the urethral glands, the author believes that it is secreted by the prostate gland. After intromission thrusting stops

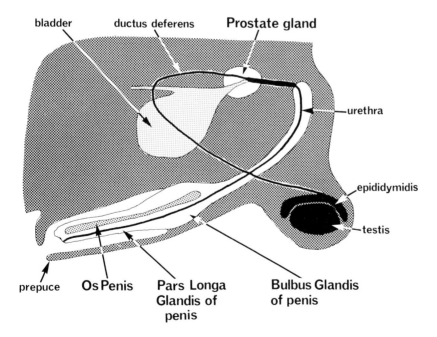

Figure 8 Reproductive system of the dog

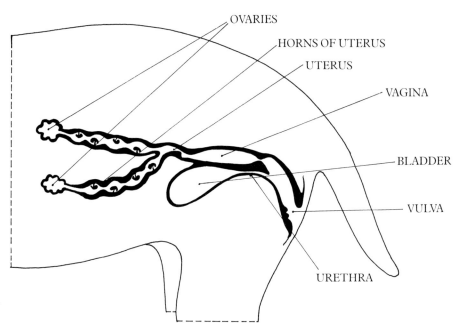

Figure 9 Reproductive system of the bitch showing the positions of seven foetuses at an early stage of growth

and the dog ejaculates the second, sperm-rich fraction; this coincides with massive enlargement and congestion of the bulbus glandis and the pars longa glandis, and an instinctive desire by the dog to turn round and achieve the classical 'copulatory tie'.

Full erection of the bulbus glandis and constriction and congestion of the vulval labiae (lips) ensure that the dog's penis remains in situ during ejaculation of the third fraction. This is a clear fluid of prostatic origin, the volume of which may exceed 15 mls, and takes up to half an hour to emit. The function of the third fraction is thought to be that of washing the second fraction, which is small in volume and is deposited in the anterior (front) vagina, into the uterine horns and eventually into the uterine tubes where fertilization occurs. In some breeds, e.g. Greyhounds, the male is sometimes not allowed to turn round completely, but as long as the penis remains in the vagina for ejaculation of the third fraction, fertility appears to be unaffected. Despite this assumption, there are many recorded instances of fertile matings occurring in the absence of a tie.

Semen Collection

There are basically two ways of collecting semen from dogs. The first is to use a piece of equipment called an artificial vagina (AV). The AV is cylindrical and lined with a soft rubber sheath. The cavity between the outer casing and the inner sheath is filled with warm water to simulate conditions in the bitch's vagina; the pressure in the water compartment can be varied by rhythmically squeezing a rubber bulb which is attached to the AV. The dog is stimulated until he gains an erection, and his penis is then guided into the AV. The ejaculate is collected in a test-tube which is attached to the AV by a rubber cone.

The second method is that of digital manipulation without an AV. This is the technique which I prefer to use for several reasons. Firstly, the AV is cumbersome and requires assistance to manipulate the instrument. This increases the number of people who are collected around the dog and may worsen his apprehension if he is nervous. Also, although it may not seem normal for the dog's penis to be uncovered during ejaculation, digital collection has never been shown to cause any psychological or physical upset, and indeed many dogs have been collected from frequently (twice weekly for over two years in our laboratory) without any noticeable effect on libido or sperm production. For those who object to digital manipulation of the dog's penis on aesthetic grounds, a certain amount of this manipulation is necessary to stimulate an erection before using the AV, and it is usually necessary to maintain digital pressure behind the bulbus glandis throughout ejaculation in both methods. It therefore appears that the grip which the bitch's vulva exerts on the base of the dog's penis during normal copulation is more important for maintaining the erection than pressure on the front part (pars longa glandis) of the penis.

In my experience, and that of some other investigators, the artificial vagina may be detrimental to sperms. This is most noticeable when collections are made from small dogs, as the AV has to be held almost horizontally under the dog's belly, and the semen is in prolonged contact with the rubber liner. This often causes a dramatic reduction in the activity of the sperms and a false impression of the dog's potential fertility.

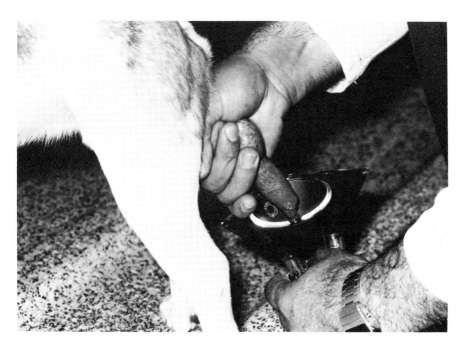

The sperm fraction of ejaculate being collected via a funnel into test-tubes

Our practice is to use a plastic test-tube and a glass funnel for collection (see photo on page 65). The dog's penis is gripped by the collector in order to induce an erection. In mature stud dogs this is easy, although in shy, inexperienced dogs it may be necessary to have a bitch in heat as a teaser. After a variable period of stimulation the dog will begin to make thrusting movements and if a bitch is present (either in or out of heat) he may try to mount. At this time the first (clear) fraction is ejaculated and no attempt is made to collect this as the dog's penis may be damaged against the collecting funnel. Cessation of thrusting coincides with ejaculation of the sperm-rich (second) fraction and an instinctive desire by the dog to turn round. This is evidenced by the dog raising one hind limb and at this time the collector deviates the dog's penis backwards (and an assistant lifts the dog's leg over the collector's arm) so that it comes to protrude between the dog's hind legs. Collection continues during this period, which lasts for only half to one minute. Then the dog recommences ejaculation of a clear fluid (the third fraction) and it is at this time that his penis reaches full erection. It is not usual for the whole of the third fraction to be collected as there are no useful tests which we can apply to this fluid in evaluating the dog's fertility.

After the dog's penis is released he may continue to ejaculate onto the floor for some time. It is best to allow him to lick his penis at this time as this will ensure that it returns to its sheath without pulling hair in. For small dogs (Chihuahuas, miniature Dachshunds and Yorkshire Terriers etc.) I have found it useful to use a small test-tube attached to a rubber cone. The problems with collecting from small breeds are related to the lack of space under the dog's abdomen and the small size of the penis. Insertion of the dog's penis into the rubber cone appears to increase the stimulation and cause ejaculation.

Insemination of the Bitch

This is a procedure which also requires simple equipment, ie a hypodermic syringe attached to a glass or plastic tube. The tube (pipette) is passed through the bitch's vulva and into the vagina to a depth of 6 – 10 cm. At this stage the tip of the pipette has reached the cervix or neck of the womb. It is virtually impossible to pass the pipette through the cervix and into the womb itself, even if a vaginoscope is used, so the semen is deposited around the cervix. It may then be an advantage to hold the bitch's hindquarters up for five to ten minutes to help the ejaculate flow forward into the uterus, or a finger may be inserted into the bitch's vagina to stimulate contractions which help to prevent backflow of semen. Walking the bitch after insemination helps to stop her from straining. In my opinion, poor conception rates after AI are probably related to our inability to deposit semen directly into the womb.

Evaluation of Semen

Our present knowledge of the causes of male infertility in dogs is limited, and the way in which we can relate sperm defects to infertility also lacks precision. The reason for our poor state of knowledge on this subject is that little effort on behalf of the veterinary profession has been directed towards it, probably because the scale of the problem appears small and funds have not been available from dog breeding organisations to support research. Less than optimal fertility in dogs is difficult to define due to the relatively low numbers of bitches which they mate, and the relatively long period of time which must elapse before it is obvious that the bitch has not conceived and is ready for mating again. Compare this with the situation in horses where a stallion may mate two or three times a day and if a mare is not pregnant she will return to heat within three weeks.

Examination of a semen sample involves the following:

(a) Assessment of motility. A quick check under the microscope will show if most of the sperms are actively moving forward. If they are it is confirmed that they are alive and it is assumed that they are capable of travelling to the uterine tubes and fertilizing an egg.

(b) Measurement of sperm numbers. Some authors express this as a percentage of sperms in the ejaculate, but this is affected by the volume of first and third fractions which is collected. A better method is to assess the concentration in the second fraction or, better still, measure the total number of sperms in the ejaculate. Although the minimum number of live sperms necessary for a fertile mating is not known, findings can be compared with recorded values for known fertile dogs. It may be many years before this problem is resolved because not only is it necessary to discover the minimum number of sperms necessary to produce conception, but in the larger breeds a figure must be found for the production of optimal litter sizes. Furthermore, it will be necessary to define more accurately the best times for inseminations.

(c) Examination of the anatomy (morphology) of the sperms. The basic classification of sperm abnormalities has been borrowed from the bull, and there is a lack of information on the relationship between sperm abnormalities and fertility in dogs. In proven animals it is assumed that the physical shape of the majority of the sperms represents the normal, and deviations from this are considered as abnormal. However, in my experience dogs producing ejaculates of normal volume and motility may show an unacceptable (arbitrarily defined as 20 per cent) number of morphologically abnormal sperms. It is then difficult, in our present state of knowledge, to be definite about a dog's potential fertility, although in such cases I always insist on a second sample being collected some time later. Another factor to be borne in mind is that the tests which we are able to employ may not be investigating all the possible reasons why sperms might be unable to effect fertilization.

Despite these problems there is one outstanding condition of male dogs which we call *spermatogenic arrest*, where a dog is fertile for a brief period but then at the age of between two and five years becomes sterile. This coincides with a decrease in the size of the testicles which become soft, although his libido (mating ability) remains good. This condition is unfortunately irreversible and there is evidence that it is inherited.

Semen Preservation

Although methods of long-term storage of semen have been evolved, the Kennel Club of Great Britain will only under special circumstances register the puppies from artificial matings when the bitch is inseminated immediately with fresh semen. However, it has been known for some years that dog semen can be diluted in various solutions and cooled to about 4°C. In this state they may be stored or transported and will remain capable of fertilization for up to four days. Recent studies on the deep-freezing of dog's semen have reached the stage where good conception rates have been achieved with semen which has been frozen for many months. But again, the use of this technique has little practical application in this country at the present time. It should also be noted that the semen of some dogs is much more fertile after freezing than others, although the reason for this is unknown.

The Application of AI

In conclusion, the main restraint on the employment of AI in the UK is a lack of request for its use, which may in some part be influenced by the attitude of the Kennel Club but is also due to many other factors. This has resulted in most veterinary practices being unable to provide an AI service because of lack of experience. It will therefore be necessary at present for most cases to be referred to the various investigation centres throughout the country. However, a sound general principal is that natural matings should be allowed and encouraged where possible, and that AI should at the present time only be considered as a last resort.

6 Pregnancy
by Dr M. J. Meredith

CHANGES OCCURRING DURING PREGNANCY

During the first month of pregnancy the bitch shows little or no outward change, but inwardly the most critical events of pregnancy are taking place. At about ten days after mating the fertilized eggs enter the uterus and after a further ten days of growth and development the embryos attach themselves to the uterine wall. At the time of attachment the embryos are like small coiled maggots, less than half an inch long − hardly auspicious of the beautiful pups they will hopefully develop into.

By five weeks after mating events are beginning to move more rapidly. The puppies have finished developing their basic shape and their vital organs and have begun the phase of a rapid increase in size (see Figure 10). The uterus has become swollen and heavy so that it rests on the floor of the abdomen. The increasing size of the uterus, particularly if the litter is large, may produce occasional signs of discomfort in the bitch and a general slowing-down of her activities. She may go off her food for a day or two, but in general her appetite increases to meet the demands of the growing litter.

The onset of changes in the teats and breasts is quite variable. In maiden bitches the teats may start to enlarge and become pink and turgid as early as four weeks after mating. In bitches which have been bred the teats are larger and may not show obvious changes until the sixth week. Swelling of the breasts becomes noticeable at around six weeks and is quite marked by seven weeks. Milk does not usually appear until a few days before whelping, although it can appear as much as two weeks before.

PSEUDOPREGNANCY (FALSE OR PHANTOM PREGNANCY)

This is a common and intriguing phenomenon in the bitch which is only rarely seen in other domesticated animals. It used to be thought that there was something wrong with a bitch which suffered false pregnancy but we now realise that this is a perfectly normal event after a season, although it is often a nuisance and at times rather alarming.

Symptoms can occur at any time between three weeks and three months after a season. One of the commonest signs is enlargement of the breasts and secretion of milk; in fact, pseudopregnant bitches are occasionally used to foster puppies. Some bitches (in my experience these are usually maidens) do not develop milk during pseudopregnancy but show only the behavioural signs. They often become strangely retiring and antisocial or even uncharacteristically aggressive. Much time is spent in their favourite bed and they may devote a lot of time to constant rearrangement of it. Distorted maternal behaviour is common and takes the form of nursing and protecting toys, slippers or other objects. In extreme cases pseudopregnant bitches can appear quite ill. They may go off their food, shiver and the exposed pink areas of skin may become pale and cold to the touch.

Do we need to worry about pseudopregnancy? Well, we now realise that pseudo-pregnancy results from normal hormone changes after a season which have the purpose of getting the uterus, breasts and maternal instincts ready for pregnancy and whelping. Affected bitches will usually get over the false pregnancy in time, but unfortunately this can take anything up to two months. If the symptoms are mild it is not too difficult to grin and bear it. An important principle is not to pander to the dog's maternal whims by letting her lie in her 'nest' for long periods or indulge in mothering her artificial puppies. This will only make her worse. It is much better to hide any 'puppies' and get her out of her bed and occupy her mind with one of her favourite games or by taking her for a walk. By this means, it is often possible to avoid the necessity for hormone treatment. People often worry a lot about the milk produced during a false pregnancy and think that treatment is essential for getting rid of it. The milk will, of course, dry up of its own accord in time, provided that you don't keep squeezing it out and hence stimulate more.

If the signs of false pregnancy are severe it will be necessary to get veterinary treatment. The behavioural changes can be very distressing both to the bitch and to the rest of the household.

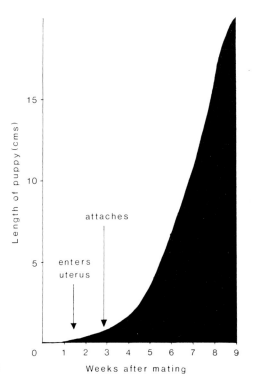

Figure 10 Growth of a puppy during pregnancy

Before leaving the subject of pseudopregnancy it may be as well to explode a few myths about it. In the first place, if a bitch suffers from false pregnancies it does not necessarily mean that she will be difficult to breed from. Secondly, breeding a bitch will not cure her of having false pregnancies and thirdly, the occurrence of false pregnancy after a season is not influenced by mating: it can occur whether she is mated or not and irrespective of the stud dog used.

PREGNANCY TESTS

Knowing whether a mating has been successful or not can be very useful from the point of view of planning litters and making arrangements for the whelping. It is also important to know whether to increase the amount fed; many bitches have become overfat as a result of feeding for a nonexistent pregnancy. There are also a number of veterinary situations when it is important to know whether or not a bitch is pregnant. From the diagnostic standpoint some of the signs of pregnancy, such as increased appetite, enlargement of the abdomen or vomiting, can also be signs of disease. From the treatment aspect there are many drugs which should be avoided during pregnancy because of the risk of abortion or damage to the developing litter. These drugs include some of the antibiotics, some insecticides and some worm treatments.

Unfortunately, there is no one hundred per cent reliable test for pregnancy in the bitch. The canine placenta does not produce the hormones which would enable blood or urine tests to be done as they are on women and mares.

Owners often place a lot of reliance on the behavioural signs of pregnancy, such as changes in temperament or activity, but as we have seen, these changes frequently occur in pseudopregnancy. The same can be said of changes in the teats and breasts. Increases in bodyweight and size of the abdomen are more useful, but again they may be due to other things such as overfeeding, reduced exercise or pyometra. On the other side of the coin, bitches with a very small litter may show no obvious size or weight changes. In the last week of pregnancy a reliable sign of the presence and health of a litter is their tiny movements against the mother's flanks when she is lying quietly.

A number of special tests for pregnancy are available. Although not perfect, they are fairly reliable provided that they are used at an appropriate stage of pregnancy. It would be nice if they could also be used to predict the number of pups but, with the possible exception of X-rays, they tend to be too inaccurate for this purpose.

Palpation

The most widely used test is palpation of the pregnant uterus at 25 to 30 days after mating. At this time the embryos themselves are too small to feel, but each embryo is surrounded by a bag of fluid resulting in a swelling in the uterus rather like a ping-pong ball (see Figure 11 overleaf) and with practice these swellings can be palpated through the flanks. In view of the risk of damaging the uterus, embryos or other abdominal structures, I would suggest that this job is best left to your veterinary surgeon who is trained and experienced in this type of work.

The accuracy of palpation depends to a large extent on the bitch. Not surprisingly,

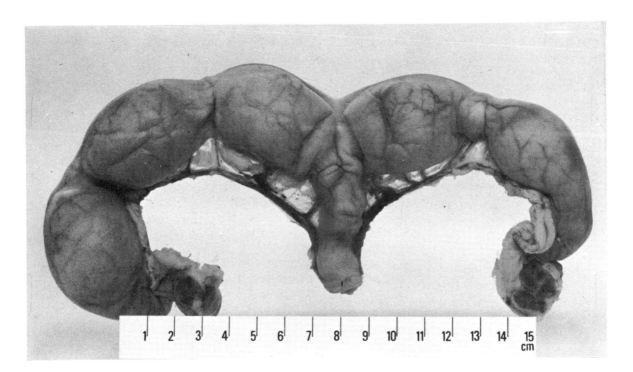

Figure 11 The pregnant uterus of a bitch at four weeks after mating. Each swelling contains an embryo suspended in a bag of fluid

the test is difficult or even impossible on fat dogs. However, just as much difficulty can arise with nervous bitches who tense their abdominal muscles like a drum. In these cases I find that prior tranquillization can be very helpful. Even when bitches are easy to examine, false diagnosis will occasionally occur. For example, the uterine swellings may be missed, particularly if only one or two are present. Sometimes the swellings lie out of reach under the rear part of the rib cage and it may be necessary to raise the forequarters of the bitch so that the uterine swellings drop back within reach. Another problem which can arise is the presence of lumps of faeces in the large intestine which may feel the right size and shape to be embryos. In spite of these difficulties, palpation is usually over 90 per cent accurate at 25 to 30 days. Beyond 30 days, palpation is much less accurate because the fluid swellings become softer and more elongated: it is then more diffcult to differentiate them from other abdominal structures. In the last two weeks of pregnancy the accuracy of palpation increases again because the pups are large enough and bony enough to be felt directly.

Scanning with ultrasound
Ultrasonic testing for pregnancy has been used on women for many years now and it is becoming increasingly popular for animals, although it is not yet widely available because of the cost of equipment and because of the experience necessary to obtain accurate results. Two basic types of instrument are available for use on animals: the Doppler type and the amplitude-depth type. The essential feature of both is a hand-held probe which emits the ultrasound and also picks up any reflected ultrasound

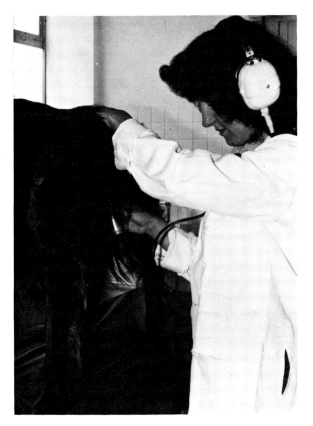 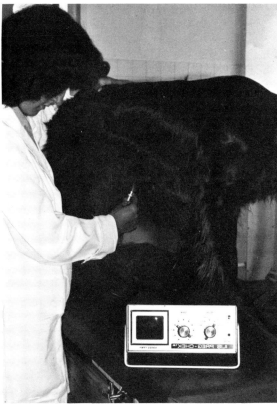

from the abdomen. The probe is held against the skin of the abdomen during scanning. The ultrasound will not travel through air so a film of oil or jelly has to be placed between the probe and the skin surface to ensure airtight contact.

The Doppler type of instrument (in use in photo above left) detects fine movements. These produce a change in frequency of reflected ultrasound which is then converted to an audible sound. In pregnancy testing we use it mainly to detect the pulse of the unborn puppies, although it will also pick up pulsations in the arteries of the mother and movements of the pups in the uterus. With this type of instrument the heartbeat or pulse of the puppies can be heard as early as five weeks after mating but a high accuracy (over 90 per cent) is not obtained until six weeks, and the accuracy of this test increases as pregnancy progresses. As a pregnancy test the Doppler instrument has the unique advantage of showing not only that the pups are there but also that they are alive and well. This can be very valuable information in cases where a bitch is showing a vaginal discharge or when there are delays or difficulties in whelping.

Amplitude-depth instruments do not give an audible output but instead have a visual display, rather like a small television screen (see photo above right), and they work by detecting the bags of fluid which surround the developing puppies. Reflect-

Left: Ultrasonic scanning for pregnancy using a Doppler instrument. Headphones are used to listen for the puppies' heartbeats

Right: Ultrasonic scanning for pregnancy using an amplitude-depth instrument. Reflections of ultrasound from the fluid surrounding the puppies appear as spikes on an oscilloscope screen

ions of ultrasound from these bags of fluid are shown as spikes on the display screen. Some skill is necessary in differentiating between the spikes of the pregnant uterus and the spikes which result from other reflections in the abdomen. One of the biggest problems comes from bladder reflections and it helps if the bitch has emptied her bladder before scanning. In experienced hands this type of instrument is over 90 per cent accurate from four weeks after mating onwards.

X-rays

The skeleton of the developing puppies begins to harden at about six weeks after mating and from seven weeks onwards it becomes visible in X-ray pictures (see below). However, taking these pictures involves exposing the bitch and puppies to large doses of radiation. As far as we can tell, the risk from this is very slight but it is probably best to avoid X-ray diagnosis of pregnancy unless it is absolutely necessary.

FEEDING

In the first month of pregnancy a bitch in good condition does not require extra food. In this period the growth of the puppies is very slight (see Figure 10) and is offset by the increased efficiency with which the bitch uses her food, due to the hormones of pregnancy. After the fourth week the growth of the puppies and of the uterus accelerates and an increasing amount of extra food will be necessary, although to some extent this is offset by the reduced activity of the bitch.

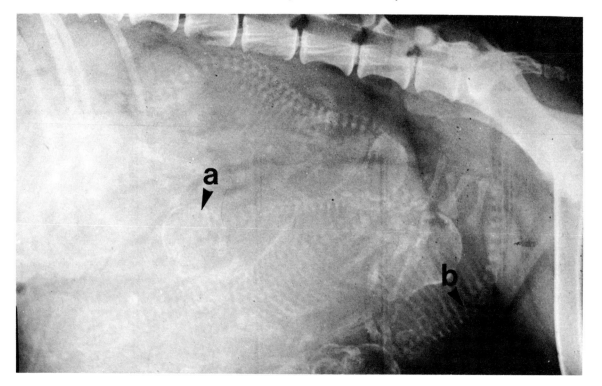

X-ray picture of the abdomen of an Irish Setter carrying thirteen puppies. (a) is the head of a puppy and (b) the backbone of a puppy

GESTATION TABLE
showing when a bitch is due to whelp

Served January	Due to whelp March	Served February	Due to whelp April	Served March	Due to whelp May	Served April	Due to whelp June	Served May	Due to whelp July	Served June	Due to whelp August	Served July	Due to whelp September	Served August	Due to whelp October	Served September	Due to whelp November	Served October	Due to whelp December	Served November	Due to whelp January	Served December	Due to whelp February
1	5	1	5	1	3	1	3	1	3	1	3	1	2	1	3	1	3	1	3	1	3	1	3
2	6	2	6	2	4	2	4	2	4	2	4	2	3	2	4	2	4	2	4	2	4	2	3
3	7	3	7	3	5	3	5	3	5	3	5	3	4	3	5	3	5	3	5	3	5	3	4
4	8	4	8	4	6	4	6	4	6	4	6	4	5	4	6	4	6	4	6	4	6	4	5
5	9	5	9	5	7	5	7	5	7	5	7	5	6	5	7	5	7	5	7	5	7	5	6
6	10	6	10	6	8	6	8	6	8	6	8	6	7	6	8	6	8	6	8	6	8	6	7
7	11	7	11	7	9	7	9	7	9	7	9	7	8	7	9	7	9	7	9	7	9	7	8
8	12	8	12	8	10	8	10	8	10	8	10	8	9	8	10	8	10	8	10	8	10	8	9
9	13	9	13	9	11	9	11	9	11	9	11	9	10	9	11	9	11	9	11	9	11	9	10
10	14	10	14	10	12	10	12	10	12	10	12	10	11	10	12	10	12	10	12	10	12	10	11
11	15	11	15	11	13	11	13	11	13	11	13	11	12	11	13	11	13	11	13	11	13	11	12
12	16	12	16	12	14	12	14	12	14	12	14	12	13	12	14	12	14	12	14	12	14	12	13
13	17	13	17	13	15	13	15	13	15	13	15	13	14	13	15	13	15	13	15	13	15	13	14
14	18	14	18	14	16	14	16	14	16	14	16	14	15	14	16	14	16	14	16	14	16	14	15
15	19	15	19	15	17	15	17	15	17	15	17	15	16	15	17	15	17	15	17	15	17	15	16
16	20	16	20	16	18	16	18	16	18	16	18	16	17	16	18	16	18	16	18	16	18	16	17
17	21	17	21	17	19	17	19	17	19	17	19	17	18	17	19	17	19	17	19	17	19	17	18
18	22	18	22	18	20	18	20	18	20	18	20	18	19	18	20	18	20	18	20	18	20	18	19
19	23	19	23	19	21	19	21	19	21	19	21	19	20	19	21	19	21	19	21	19	21	19	20
20	24	20	24	20	22	20	22	20	22	20	22	20	21	20	22	20	22	20	22	20	22	20	22
21	25	21	25	21	23	21	23	21	23	21	23	21	22	21	23	21	23	21	23	21	23	21	22
22	26	22	26	22	24	22	24	22	24	22	24	22	23	22	24	22	24	22	24	22	24	22	24
23	27	23	27	23	25	23	25	23	25	21	25	23	24	23	25	23	25	23	25	23	25	23	25
24	28	24	28	24	26	24	26	24	26	24	26	24	25	24	26	24	26	24	26	24	26	24	25
25	29	25	29	25	27	25	27	25	27	25	27	25	26	25	27	25	27	25	27	25	27	25	26
26	30	26	30	26	28	26	28	26	28	26	28	26	27	26	28	26	28	26	28	26	28	26	27
27	31	27	1 (April)	27	29	27	29	27	29	27	29	27	28	27	29	27	29	27	29	27	29	27	28
28	1 (April)	28	2	28	30	28	30	28	30	28	30	28	29	28	30	28	30	28	30	28	30	28	1 (March)
29	2	29	3	29	31	29	1 (July)	29	31	29	31	29	30	29	31	29	31	29	31	29	31	29	2
30	3			30	1 (June)	30	2	30	1 (Aug.)	30	1 (Sept.)	30	1 (Oct.)	30	1 (Nov.)	30	2 (Dec.)	30	1 (Jan.)	30	1 (Feb.)	30	3
31	4			31	2			31	2			31	2	31	2			31	2			31	4

Month labels printed in the table to indicate the change of whelping month: May, April, July, June, March, June, Aug., Sept., Oct., Nov., Dec., Jan., Feb.

A guide to the amount of extra feeding is to increase the food gradually from four weeks so that the bitch is getting one-third extra each day by five weeks and 50 per cent extra just before term. For large breeds as much as two-thirds extra food may be necessary in the last week of pregnancy. As with any feeding advice the ultimate criterion is the condition of the bitch. If she is allowed to become too lean or too fat this can result in problems with whelping and rearing.

In the last month of pregnancy the swollen uterus will be taking up much of the room in the abdomen and leaving less room for expansion of the stomach. For this reason it is advisable to divide the food up into at least three meals a day. Fresh water should, of course, be constantly available.

Many owners give mineral or vitamin supplements to the pregnant bitch. If you are feeding a balanced diet this is unnecessary. People often do not realise that these extra minerals and vitamins can actually be harmful, either by direct toxic effect (e.g. vitamins A and D) or, more commonly, by reducing the availability of vitamins and minerals which are not included in the supplement. From the point of view of feeding a balanced diet, there is much to be said for using a commercial tinned or soft-moist diet from a reputable manufacturer. This may not give the same artistic satisfaction as making up your own diet but the commercial foods have been extensively researched and tested and are a much safer proposition. In my opinion, the only reasons for giving nutritional supplements are: medical problems in the bitch, poor appetite and possibly for giant breeds. In these cases it is wise to discuss the use of suitable supplements with your veterinary surgeon.

EXERCISE

Regular exercise is important during pregnancy to maintain health and to keep the muscles in tone ready for whelping. However, strenuous exercise and rough games should be avoided. Working dogs should be excused duties beyond the fourth week. If dogs are worked in late pregnancy there is a risk of damage to the swelling teats and breasts and a risk of torsion of the uterus. Another consideration is that if any limb injuries occur it will be more difficult to get them right at a time when they have an increased load to carry.

PROBLEMS ASSOCIATED WITH PREGNANCY

Vomiting is probably the commonest problem during pregnancy. Pregnant bitches do not suffer from 'morning sickness' in the same way that pregnant women can but they do have mechanical problems resulting from the pressure of the pregnant uterus on the stomach. Often this can be prevented by giving smaller meals but if it should persist then a veterinary examination is advisable.

Pregnancy failure can occur at any stage from the time of conception until the time of whelping. The reasons for pregnancy failure in the bitch are largely unknown. Severe stress or injury can result in pregnancy failure but it is often surprising how some bitches suffer stress or injury during pregnancy and yet go on to whelp normally. If pregnancy fails during the first month, then there is unlikely to be any external indication. The term 'resorption' is commonly used to refer to pregnancy failure without any obvious expulsion of pups or their membranes, but in my view this term is best avoided because it is very doubtful that the uterus is capable of absorbing the complex molecules present in the pups and their membranes. It is more likely that the developing pups degenerate within the uterus and are then expelled into the lower genital tract from where they will probably be washed out in the urine. Developing puppies and their membranes are largely composed of water so there will be very little solid material to notice when the degenerate remnants are expelled. Because of this absence of external signs, it is impossible to know whether the reason for a bitch not whelping is that she had a pregnancy which failed during the early stages, or because she never became pregnant in the first place. Even if the bitch was diagnosed as pregnant, we still cannot be certain that she was because none of the tests available is one hundred per cent accurate.

If pregnancy fails later than one month after mating it is much more likely that the expelled remnants will be obvious and recognisable, particularly after six weeks when the skeleton begins to harden. A pregnancy failure which leads to expulsion of recognisable puppies is termed *abortion*.

The possibility of abortion is always a worry with the pregnant bitch. The first sign is a green, brown or blood-stained discharge from the vagina. Not all discharges indicate that the bitch is going to abort: white or yellow discharge usually indicates a vaginal infection. *Vaginal infection* is not uncommon during pregnancy but it is a cause for concern because there is always a risk that it may spread to the uterus or to the puppies during the birth process. In any case of vaginal discharge, persistent vomiting or loss of appetite for more than a day or two, it is wise to seek veterinary attention.

Worming. In the past people have often advised routine worming during pregnancy in the mistaken belief that it would prevent the bitch passing worms to her pups. We now know that none of the drugs we have available can stop a bitch transmitting roundworms to her pups although a drug called fenbendazole (marketed as Panacur) has recently been shown to have some activity against dormant stages of roundworms if it is given for a five day period prior to day 50 of pregnancy. Worming her will remove any worms from her intestines but it will not touch the dormant stages lying elsewhere in her body which pass into the unborn pups in late pregnancy. The best time to worm the bitch is before mating and then again when the suckling pups are old enough to be treated.

7 Whelping

As already indicated, although the 'official' period of gestation is sixty-three days it is not abnormal for the bitch to whelp at fifty-eight days or hang on for as long as sixty-nine days after mating. The complexity of the process is such that it is impossible to work out exact dates for any stage of the whelping process. Keep in the forefront of your mind that all the times given in this chapter are approximations only. Note carefully each stage and only start to worry if events differ markedly from the outline given here. Remember that real pain and evidence of approaching exhaustion are your most reliable indicators that things are not proceeding according to plan. Read Chapter 8 on the Problems of Parturition carefully so that you are aware of what could go wrong, but do not forget that most whelpings are both easy and trouble-free and that your vet is only a telephone call away.

Final Preparations

By the seventh week of pregnancy your bitch should be comfortably installed in her whelping box. It is important to give her plenty of time to get used to new surroundings if she is to have her puppies away from her normal sleeping quarters, so please do not leave the arrangements until the last minute. In fact, bitches like to find somewhere private for the birth of their puppies and, with luck, she will decide that her whelping box is enough of a change and safe enough to have a litter in. I do not suppose for a moment that this will prevent her from spending a few days digging about in the garden but she may not take her search for seclusion quite so seriously if she has a quiet, warm and dark place already provided!

By seven weeks she will be giving an excellent impression of a canine tank and it is particularly important that she does not receive any bumps or knocks. (Most bitches are very aware of their increased size, but some imagine that they are as sylph-like as ever and try to squeeze through the gaps and doors just as they did before they were mated.) By this time, too, she will be receiving two or even three small meals a day totalling approximately half as much again as she normally eats. This is per *day* not per meal: please do not be tempted to overfeed her. There will be much more pressure on her bladder during the last two weeks and she will probably need to urinate more often. Many bitches, however clean they normally are, cannot last overnight at this time. I lay paper down for mine which they use if they are pushed. I do not scold them – they really cannot help it.

The First Stage of Whelping

About twenty-four hours before they are going to whelp some bitches will refuse their food. This is often quoted as an infallible means of predicting the onset of parturition — but as all my bitches invariably eat hearty meals until the last moment I do not find this method very useful! More helpful is the scratching, digging and general restlessness which always accompany the first stage of labour. This period can easily last up to forty-eight hours so there is no point in getting anxious at this stage or sitting around and waiting for the first puppy. You can use the time productively by making sure that the coat is clipped around her teats if she is long-coated and that the general area of the undercarriage is kept clean and, perhaps, washed with a mild disinfectant.

If you have a complicated garden with shrubberies and sheds do make sure that you keep a close eye on her while she is outside. Despite that beautiful, clean, warm whelping box into which you thought she was so contentedly settled, she might well take it into her head that a dirty hole underneath a thick bramble bush is much more satisfactory. I have a friend who had to dig out the foundations of her garage to retrieve a bitch who had been secretly arranging her own quarters, safe, snug and totally inaccessible to a human being! Another point to watch is that the place you have set aside for the whelping room is not one to which other dogs or your cat have access — even the most placid of bitches may resent the intrusion of an outsider.

If you are very well organised or you are particularly anxious to know when the litter is going to arrive, you could check your bitch's temperature for the week or so preceeding the time she is due. Take it regularly each morning and evening, preferably in the same place and after she has lain quietly for ten minutes. The most reliable indicator of the time of whelping is the sharp drop in temperature which almost always occurs within twenty-four hours of the onset of the second stage. One of the confusing things about the first stage is that the bitch will do a lot of panting. This comes in spasms and if you have not whelped a bitch before it is easy to imagine that they are contractions. (Once you have seen true contractions you cannot mistake them!) What is happening at the panting stage is that the cervix, which is at the neck of the uterus, is dilating (relaxing) and the puppies are changing their position — hopefully to head down — in preparation for their journey along the uterine horns. The vulva, already rather large and puffy, becomes very moist and open and begins to excrete a thick white or creamy discharge. Should there be a dark, bloodstained, green or purilent discharge at this stage you should contact your vet.

Despite all this 'keeping an eye' and 'taking care', try not to fuss your bitch too much. A maiden bitch, particularly one kept as a house pet, will be very sensitive to your moods, tensions and anxieties and she may actually prevent whelping taking place if she feels insecure or worried. Try to remain calm and matter-of-fact and be as normal as possible, however tense you feel. Before the second stage of labour begins there may be some quite long periods when your bitch is perfectly relaxed. Forty-eight hours is two whole days so spend the time calmly ensuring that you have got in everything that you need.

The Second Stage

The second stage begins with the first main contraction. If at all possible make a note of this time as, should there be any complications, your vet will want to know how long the bitch has been straining. Although some bitches make much more of a performance over whelping than others, the contractions are quite unmistakable. The whole body tenses up from shoulder to rump and you can almost see the muscles squeezing from the ribs backwards. Each puppy is wrapped in two layers of tough membrane and protected by a cushioning of fluid and is attached to the placenta (which looks rather like a small liver, although is can be nearly as big as the puppy) which is itself attached to the wall of the uterine horn. The placenta acts as a combined filter and store – during pregnancy it performs the functions of liver and kidneys and during birth it holds a supply of nutrients and oxgenated blood which will keep the pup alive until its own system functions for itself. The contractions produce a hydraulic-like movement along the horns which forces the puppies along the canal towards the pelvic inlet (though, perhaps, 'outlet' would be a better expression in this case!).

The shape of the pelvis and the position of the whelps in most breeds is such that the puppies have to climb over a 'hump' before they can descend through the pelvis. The contractions are therefore very powerful and consume a great deal of energy. As each puppy reaches the top of the hump the contractions come more regularly until the whelp slides out. During the latter part of the journey the outer membrane breaks, the fluid is released and exits from the vulva in a rush. This is quite normal as it has completed its job by this time and the bag containing the whelp can then come through more easily because it is not so large. The fluid is a dirty, dark green colour and its arrival usually means that the pup is not far behind. If the bag does not burst the front end of it sometimes emerges, filled with liquid, with the puppy still inside the vagina. There is a moment of panic as you imagine that the bag is empty but it usually means that despite the imminent arrival of the whelp the muscles around the vulva are not yet fully relaxed and a little help is required as explained later.

The process is repeated for each of the whelps and there are not usually any problems unless a whelp is much too big (a rather more common occurrence in small breeds, particularly those which have been bred down), two arrive at exactly the same time or there is some sort of malpresentation. Under normal circumstances the first whelp will be born between half an hour and an hour after the second stage begins. If the first one takes much longer than this, and certainly if she strains longer than two hours you should contact your vet.

The whelp will usually arrive still encased inside the inner membrane and its struggles trigger the bitch to bite at the membrane and free the puppy. Occasionally a puppy arrives without its protecting bag but this is no cause for alarm as the bitch may have split it as the puppy dropped from the vulva or it will have broken slightly earlier and the placenta will bring it through. The placenta almost always comes immediately after the whelp and is still attached to the puppy's tummy by the umbilical cord. In a few breeds the placenta is regularly retained until many hours after the whelping – English Setters are one example. No one seems to know the reason for this but there is certainly a tendency for such breeds to be subject to a haemorrhage subsequent to whelping so keep a careful eye on them. It is a good idea to keep a count of the placentas just in case one has remained behind but, given the opportunity, the

'Something is definitely beginning to happen'

'I had better have a closer look'

'One more squeeze I think'

'That's one out!'

'I don't really need help
with this membrane'

'I am quite capable of
dealing with the placenta
myself'

'This needs a good clean'

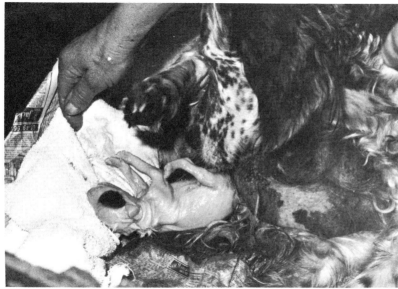

'Now, a towel is what I call sensible – and look at that black eye!'

bitch will eat them all and you will probably miss one or two. My breed has relatively small litters so I usually let them have the placentas as they are very rich in nutrients, but where the litters are large I would not think it wise to allow her to eat more than half of them or she will be uncomfortably loose for a few days.

A maiden bitch is sometimes not quite sure what to do. If she does not seem to be confident, thoroughly scrub your hands and split the membrane around the puppy, making sure that you remove any mucus from in and around its mouth. As already explained, from the time the placenta comes away from the uterine wall the supply of oxygen within the bloodstream of the whelp is strictly limited so it is important to make the puppy breathe as soon as possible. The bitch usually does this by rolling the pup around while she is licking it clean and cutting through the umbilical cord but you may have to help by giving it a good shake. You will soon hear a little gasp and a

'There's food here
somewhere'

cry and this means all is well. Once the dam hears that cry even the most reluctant
bitch will usually take over her pup and, after the first one, she should have no further
reservations. If for any reason (and bitches can think of many good ones even if we do
not understand them) she has had her first puppy in the wrong place, just putting the
pup into her whelping box will almost certainly make her settle down.

I like to cut the cord myself if I can as there is a tendency for the bitch to nick it off
rather short if left to herself. Some breeders advise that the cord should be tied off to
ensure that no blood is lost, or that it should be torn rather than cut but I have never
found any problems with just snipping it with a pair of scissors about two inches from
the navel. Once the bitch gets the hang of it she may begin to break the cords as the
pup leaves her body. The placenta will follow almost immediately anyway.

Most whelps will begin to wriggle and kick very soon after birth. The dam will lick
them, roll them over and push them about generally and it is not usually long before
the puppy is struggling towards its mother's teats. Occasionally a puppy is born and
remains quite still. Under these circumstances the dam will sometimes ignore it completely as movement seems to be necessary in the whelp to trigger their instinctive
behaviour. Either way, if the pup seems limp and lifeless the relatively gentle treatment that it will receive from its mother is unlikely to start it breathing. Before you
start to revive the whelp examine it carefully to make sure that it is fully formed.
Check the roof of the mouth particularly, as incomplete formation of the palate is
often an indication of other abnormalities and in such cases it is pointless to revive the
pup. However, if apart from its lifelessness the puppy seems sound, do anything
necessary to revive it: wrap it in a rough towel and rub the body vigorously, making

sure that the head is supported, shake it very hard, pump at its ribs, blow into its mouth, place a couple of drops of brandy onto its tongue, swing it round and round in the towel. Do not give up – really work at it. I have jumped about upwards of fifteen minutes on a puppy which eventually coughed and spluttered and started to struggle. Believe me, it is worth it – they have grown up as strong and healthy as the rest of the litter. If you succeed, place the pup back with its mother and hope for the best. Most bitches will take over without any problems, but if she will not accept it refer to Chapter 9.

After the birth of the first puppy there is a pause before the next one comes along; this can be as short as ten minutes or as long as four hours. Some bitches will have a puppy or two and then relax and even sleep for a couple of hours before having the next. The time between whelps is less significant than the time the bitch is actually straining. Again, an absolute maximum of two hours' straining is all that you should allow before consulting your vet. Occasionally, a bitch might wait twenty-four hours before producing her final whelp, although in these cases the puppy is almost always born dead.

During whelping and just after, it is very unlikely that your bitch will want food. She is, on the other hand, very likely to be thirsty so water, with glucose and a little milk added, should always be available. Offer it to her regularly – despite her thirst

Just beginning to get crowded – and it looks as if there's another one coming

she may not be prepared to leave her puppies for even a moment. You will have the same problem a little later when she needs to relieve herself − even after she has been forcibly put outside she may be so anxious to return that she will not perform. Leave her until she does, though. She will be a lot more comfortable afterwards and it gives you time to have a proper clean-up of her whelping box, replacing the layers of soiled paper and putting in the pad of SnugRug or Vetbed. You can also take your time over the examination of the puppies. Carefully check for deformities and make sure each of them can suck successfully. You can do this by pushing your well-scrubbed little finger into the puppy's mouth. If you cannot feel it pulling on your finger something is wrong and if you have not previously seen a cleft palate you should consult your vet. You may, regretfully, have to cull and these should be removed from the litter while the bitch is out of the way and taken to your veterinary surgeon who will put them to sleep quickly, and painlessly. It is sensible to do what has to be done straight away − there is nothing worse than listening to a puppy cry and whimper its way to death because it is unable to suck or is not strong enough to compete with its fellows for milk.

Snags during Whelping

Most whelpings progress smoothly but there are occasional snags which you can over-come yourself without pressing the panic button and calling out your vet. Most are dealt with fully in the next chapter but, if you feel confident, there are one or two things you can try which could save trouble. The best way for a whelp to be presented is headfirst, although nearly half are born the other way round and give no trouble. Sometimes a whelp is a bit too big, the bitch is not producing quite enough fluid or has not relaxed her various muscles enough and the result is that the pup gets stuck. Very often you can solve the problem yourself by giving the dam some help.

If she has been pushing hard for over an hour give yourself a good surgical scrub and, leaving your hand still wet, lubricate it with the KY jelly. Stand the bitch up and carefully insert two fingers into the vagina, sliding them up towards the tail − as you will see from the diagrams the birth canal drops down to the vulva from the pelvic inlet. Crooking your fingers, pull the channel back. This will induce the bitch to strain and, if the whelp is in the birth canal, you should be able to feel it pushing down. If the problem is one of size, lubrication or muscular tension and the puppy has got over the pelvic 'hump', you can introduce jelly into the canal and gradually stretch the muscles round the whelp. This is not something that can be done quickly and you should only try it if you are confident that you can manage it. You may not succeed, of course, but, so long as your hands are absolutely clean and you are very gentle, you are not likely to do any harm. The presence of your fingers inside the vagina will keep the bitch straining. As she pushes, gradually move your fingers round the whelp, stretching the opening and introducing the jelly. Do *not*, under any circumstances, try to get hold of the puppy. If it will not come with the help you are giving it you need your vet. Once the front half of the pup is out of the vulva you can gently wrap it in a towel and ease it carefully downwards. Do not twist as this could cause considerable damage. If in doubt − stop and call your vet.

Incidentally, your veterinary surgeon may come to you, but it is often quicker for you to go to him. There is always the possibility of a caesarean so you might just as well be where all the equipment is. Make sure that you have a large box for the puppies in the car as well as a hot-water bottle and plenty of old blankets for wrapping up and supporting the bitch afterwards. Another advantage is that the journey can often trigger off the necessary contractions. You would not be the first to arrive at the vet's with a couple of puppies which you did not have when you started out!

Aftermath

When it is all over the bitch should settle down with her pups quite contentedly. It is sometimes difficult to tell when she has finished whelping but her overall manner − relaxed, sleeping, or allowing her puppies to feed without disturbing them by continually shifting position − is the best guide. She will also be beginning to feel hungry so make sure that she has something light and easily digestible. Milk pudding, chicken or egg custard are ideal foods − she deserves something a bit special. After all that, with luck, you can both get some rest.

Before this chapter is concluded I feel that it is only right to say something about culling. It is to be hoped that no one would allow their bitch to have a litter unless they were confident that they were able to find good homes for the puppies. This applies to crossbred and mongrel litters just as much as to those of pedigree dogs. However, if your bitch has been mismated or has a very large litter and there is little prospect of the pups being sold it is absolutely essential that the surplus is destroyed as soon as possible after whelping. Nature being what it is there will always be some weaklings in any large litter. The longer the decision is left the harder it will be to take and your vet will be happier if you bring them in early. The dog population of the UK already exceeds our requirements by many hundreds of thousands and it is needless cruelty to keep whelps alive if they are likely to end up being passed from family to family, allowed to run wild or spend most of their unhappy lives in a rescue kennel. The bitch will be just as happy with three as she will with nine, so long as they are removed early and tactfully. If you cannot be firm with yourself − and your family − at this stage you should not have started.

8 Problems of Parturition
by J. O. Joshua

Although everyone recognises that the state of parturition (giving birth) is an entirely natural one, there must be few experienced breeders − possibly excluding those who breed dogs for commercial gain only, the so-called 'puppy farmers' − who would not admit to the occasional twinge of anxiety as any bitch in their possession approaches the time for whelping. Whilst some problems can be anticipated with varying degrees of apprehension even the easiest whelper in the kennel can run into a 'once-off' problem, such as a malpresentation.

To understand the problems some knowledge of a few points is helpful.

The process of giving birth is customarily divided into three stages, in any one of which some abnormality can arise.

Stage 1. The stage of relaxation and dilation of the cervix. The muscles of the uterus are never in a state of complete inactivity and during late pregnancy they become more active and are in a state of rhythmic contraction which is neither felt by the bitch nor can it be seen by an observer. As the time of whelping approaches these contractions become strong enough to force the fluid-filled foetal membranes (after-birth) against the still-closed cervix. Increasing hydraulic pressure causes the gradual opening of the cervix.

During this phase bitches show discomfort (pain is not a marked feature) and apprehension; they are restless, indulge in increasingly vigorous bed-making and have periods of shivering and panting.

The duration of the first stage is exceedingly variable, from where none is apparent at all, ie the bitch which drops a pup without warning and to everyone's surprise, up to a duration of forty-eight hours, although this is unusually long and perhaps should be regarded as not normal. Between six and twenty-four hours can be regarded as normal.

The important thing is that the signs of stage 1 should become increasingly strong until in the later stages visible abdominal straining (labour pains, bearing-down) can be seen. Failure of this crescendo to occur will be discussed later.

Stage 2. The stage of actual expulsion of the puppies during which time vigorous straining efforts should be seen, with rest intervals between each birth.

These intervals again vary considerably, from five minutes to four hours although once again the latter figure is verging on the abnormal. Ten to thirty minute intervals are certainly normal. Several pups may be born with this sort of interval between; sometimes the whole litter is delivered at such regular intervals, but it is neither unusual nor abnormal for there to be a resting interval of one to three hours followed by the birth of several more pups.

Stage 3. The stage of expulsion of the foetal membranes. In animals which normally have one offspring, e.g. the cow, the afterbirth is expelled within a few hours after the infant arrives, but in species such as the dog and cat stage 3 is normally repeated with each birth.

The following are all normal for the bitch:

a) Birth of the puppy still enclosed in its intact membranes.

b) The membranes have ruptured and the extremity of the puppy is exposed but the afterbirth remains attached by the umbilical cord and is expelled immediately.

c) The membranes rupture and either the umbilical cord breaks as the pup is born or the bitch bites it through as soon as she can reach it; in this case the membranes may remain in the uterus or vagina. As a rule this set will be expelled before the birth of the next puppy, but sometimes two or more further whelps arrive before more afterbirths are seen in which case several sets are expelled at one time.

Abnormalities of this stage will be discussed later.

Normal whelping must depend on the proper structure and function of all the parts concerned and on a correct relationship between them. For example, the muscles of the uterus must be able to contract rhythmically and vigorously if puppies are to be propelled towards, into and through the birth canal. On the other hand a vigorous uterus is useless if the cervix does not dilate at the right time, or if the bony part of the birth canal is too small or is deformed. Lastly, if all these things are right but the puppy is too large or is not in a correct position for normal birth, then again there may be trouble.

Just to confuse matters further there are numerous variations which occur in the dog, probably more so than in any other species; the following are some examples.

ANATOMY

Because of the wide variation in breeds it is not possible to regard dogs just as a single, simple species having a basic anatomical makeup for which normal values can be given. On a weight basis alone the variables are almost infinite, from one-and-a-half to two hundred pounds at extreme ends of the scale. Hence, the use of pelvimetry (the technique of measuring pelvic dimensions), which is freely used in human obstetrics, is just not on in the dog.

All that a veterinary surgeon can do when asked to examine a bitch for suitability for breeding as regards the pelvis is to make a digital examination via a finger in the rectum to assess the size and contours of the pelvic inlet and then to base his advice on knowledge of the breed in question, especially as regards the range of puppy size to be expected. In breeds where smallness is a desirable show feature and the process of miniaturisation is a relatively modern one (say within the last fifty to one hundred years) marked variation in size of the foetus is common.

True, X-ray examination can be used to outline the pelvis, but it can achieve little that the experienced finger cannot and may even be misleading. Also the use of X-rays during pregnancy should be avoided whenever possible.

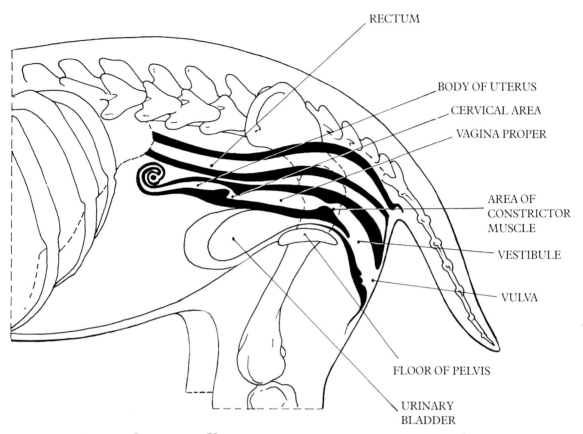

Figure 12 Normal birth canal

LENGTH OF VAGINA

The vagina of the bitch, which comprises two parts: the vestibule nearer to the vulva and the vagina proper, mainly within the pelvis, is extremely long, e.g. in a twenty-five pound bitch (small Cocker or large Welsh Corgi size) the length of the vagina is in the range 10 – 14 cm. There are few people with a finger even 10 cm long hence it is quite impossible to reach the cervix (neck of the womb) in any except very small bitches, or occasionally in medium-sized bitches it may be reached during a maximum straining effort when she is in labour.

This factor presents considerable problems in diagnosis in certain forms of dystokia (difficult birth), especially in uterine inertia cases when one is trying to ascertain whether stage 2 of labour has commenced. Since positive diagnosis of stage 2 depends on being able to ascertain whether the cervix is fully dilated it becomes a trifle difficult when it cannot possibly be reached! The use of a vaginal speculum in a whelping bitch is not really practical and in any event could seldom be justified for a variety of reasons.

VARIATION IN WHELPING PATTERNS

Veterinary surgeons are often asked how long it is safe to leave a bitch in labour before seeking professional advice if no progress is evident. There is no simple, single answer to this one either, although some limits can be defined.

The difficulty is that normal whelping varies so widely from breed to breed; what may be normal in one may be quite abnormal in another.

As a general rule, bitches of larger breeds which usually produce large litters are easier and quicker whelpers than small breeds having smaller litters. The reason for this lies mainly in the ratio of foetal size to dam's body size, e.g. if a bitch has a litter of ten puppies the average birthweight of individuals will be less than that of a similar-sized bitch of a breed which normally produces four or five pups only. Thus less effort is required to expel a relatively small puppy in a larger litter than a bigger puppy in a small litter.

With the exception of the few really flat-faced breeds, the shape of the foetal head is surprisingly similar. However, the foetal head in breeds such as the Pekinese is round and less conical and is therefore not so easily engaged in the pelvic inlet and this may prolong the early part of second-stage labour.

The force and vigour of straining also varies and it is necessary for owners to have some idea of what is normal, not only in their breed but in their particular strain. An example which comes to mind is the Chihuahua. Many of these little bitches are very forceful whelpers and they strain extremely vigorously; the importance of this fact is that it may be necessary to obtain help at a much earlier stage than in a bitch which is comparatively sluggish in her straining efforts.

Boxers may be most misleading in that their posterior vagina is so large and relaxed that they seem to be making little effort, yet on examination one finds that the pup is just about to slide out with the greatest of ease!

These few examples are mentioned to illustrate the point that it is simply not possible to lay down hard and fast rules of timing and normality but these will be referred to later under the various headings.

Dystokia or Difficult Birth

It is customary to divide causes of dystokia into two broad categories of maternal and foetal. Obviously this implies that maternal causes are due to some structural or functional abnormality of the dam, whereas foetal causes arise from the shape, size or posture of the whelp.

MATERNAL CAUSES OF DYSTOKIA

1) The pelvis
If the pelvis is deformed in any way it may cause some obstruction to the passage of a puppy through the birth canal. The commonest cause of deformity is fracture of the pelvis in a street accident, and it should be remembered that even in the best-regulated circles a bitch in season may escape and get herself run over!

From the functional point of view even severe fractures of the pelvis heal quite astonishingly well and the dog may even become show-ring sound again, but deformity nearly always results which will make whelping difficult or impossible and this is one time when what is called an elective caesarean section is called for.

It is said that severe rickets in puppyhood will cause deformity of the pelvis leading to whelping problems. I have never been convinced of the validity of this theory in the dog, although I have seen such cases in the cat. I cannot recall seeing it in a bitch.

2) The vagina

Older bitches may develop tumours in the vagina, usually not malignant, and these can become an obstruction to whelping. The presence of the tumours may not even be suspected until trouble arises at whelping. Both 1) and 2) will cause trouble of the type known as obstructive dystokia; here the bitch is trying to push her pups through a narrowed birth canal.

The signs the owner is most likely to see is the bitch straining vigorously but no evidence that a puppy is advancing into the visible part of the vagina. How soon should the owner ask for help? It is impossible to be absolutely precise but if the bitch is really straining forcibly and regularly it is wise to alert your veterinary surgeon after an hour has passed without progress; certainly do not leave it longer than two hours without reporting possible problems. It may well be that you will be advised to wait a little longer and to make a further report – there are so many factors your veterinary surgeon will need to take into account.

3) General conformation

Desired show points in some breeds may result in a body shape which is not conducive to easy whelping. I would class the Bulldog and Pekinese amongst these. In both the desired conformation leads to a large front end and much smaller and narrower hindquarters which often denotes a small pelvis. Not all bitches in these breeds have a small pelvis, in some it is surprisingly roomy, but in many the pelvic inlet is small when one considers the size of puppies expected to pass through it.

In the Bulldog the light hindquarters may produce a 'waist' effect, and in the heavily pregnant bitch the laden uterus will fall well below the line of the pelvis so that, in effect, the whelps have to climb up a steep slope before they can get into the pelvic inlet and, even then, may be at the wrong angle when they get there.

In these cases straining may not be as vigorous as anticipated because the puppy head is not engaging in the pelvis and this engagement of the head is one of the main factors in promoting vigorous straining efforts. Whatever the cause, the absence of strong and regular contractions makes it wise to seek veterinary advice when no progress from first stage labour is seen.

4) A small, unrelaxed vulva

This is not common but occasionally occurs. As a rule the vulva of a pregnant bitch remains a little larger than before she came into season and even if this is not obvious some relaxation of the vulva will occur, due to hormonal changes, when whelping is imminent.

In cases such as these, normal progress is made and the first puppy can be seen or felt distending the vagina below the anus, but the presenting part does not appear. The bitch shows more pain than average and often cries out. It is sometimes possible gently to stretch the lips of the vulva and help the head (or hind end) through; once the first pup has been born there is seldom further trouble. On very rare occasions it is necessary to perform episiotomy (surgical incision of the vulva) to permit birth of the pup; needless to say this is a job for the veterinary surgeon.

5) Nervous inhibition of labour

This sounds a formidable title but all it means is that, owing to some form of stress, often mental stress, the bitch does not relax and can actually prevent the progress of labour either from stage 1 to stage 2, or she can even interrupt the second stage and call a halt to proceedings.

Many factors can cause stress:

a) Basic temperament, ie the bitch is neurotic. This is most common in pet bitches which have often sublimated their maternal instincts in their attachment to their owners and what should be an essentially natural process becomes the cause of unreasonable apprehension resulting in an unduly protracted and distressing first-stage labour. Some bitches are almost hysterical in their reaction to first-stage labour. Very mild tranquillizers may be necessary but should not be administered without veterinary advice as to choice of drug and dosage.

b) 'Unsuitable' environment for the whelping. I have put 'unsuitable' in quotes because often the whelping place is eminently suitable as judged by the objective observer and provides everything required but is *not* acceptable to the individual most concerned, the bitch! Sudden change of environment, no matter how well-meaning, may cause a bitch to refuse to whelp. Oddly enough it can be just as bad to bring a kennel bitch into the house as it is to consign the cossetted household pet to a garage or garden shed.

We are also all familiar with the bitch who makes her own choice of whelping place, whether it be in a totally inaccessible spot under a balcony or shed or on the best bed with the newest eiderdown.

Thus a great deal of tact and understanding may be needed to persuade a bitch to get down to it in the place you have deemed most suitable. I have even been reduced to covering the chosen bed and eiderdown with waterproof sheeting and allowing the bitch to whelp there, transferring her to the 'proper' place when whelping was completed.

c) Disturbance during labour. Any unusual disturbance can cause a bitch to stop whelping, even when some pups are already born. One example is an invited 'audience' – this may sound unbelievable but I have seen it happen. A Boxer patient of mine proceeded to whelp three puppies very easily and then stopped – no straining, no nothing. After about three hours the owner phoned me and on making careful enquiry I found she was virtually holding a coffee morning in the kitchen (where the bitch was), the whelping being an added attraction. My comments and instructions were terse and pointed; when I arrived fifteen minutes later the bitch was alone and had already produced two further pups. She completed her whelping easily and undisturbed.

Whilst unobtrusive observation is essential, to make a whelping bitch a public entertainment is deplorable. And don't say things of this sort don't happen in 'our' world of dog breeding. What about the exhibitors who have taken whelping bitches to shows so that they wouldn't miss a chance of another red card?

6) Uterine inertia

Although last in order of writing under this heading this is very far from being the least important condition, indeed it is one of the more common causes of whelping problems.

The immediate cause is an inability of the muscles of the uterus to contract sufficiently to expel the whelps in a reasonable time, ie the muscles are inert.

Why this should occur is not precisely understood, there are probably several factors involved. Almost certainly hormonal factors play a part but to some extent mechanical conditions also have to be considered. Inertia is often present when the number of foetuses is below average, especially in what we call single-foetus pregnancies, but inertia can also very occasionally occur in extremely heavily pregnant bitches. In the former category the uterine muscle is not sufficiently stretched to respond to the hormonal changes at whelping time, in the latter the muscle is so over-stretched that it simply cannot contract until the pressure in the womb is slightly reduced by the assisted delivery of one or two pups. However, it must not be thought that bitches pregnant with a normal, average number of pups will not suffer from inertia, indeed they do.

A disturbing feature is that there is an indoubted tendency for inertia to occur in families, hence it must be accepted that heredity plays some part. Strains showing a high incidence of inertia should be discarded from the breeding programme. I have done just this myself, so I have practised what I preach.

Inertia is subdivided in several ways, but this is mainly of importance to the veterinary surgeon. However, all degrees of inertia exist, from the severest form, complete primary inertia when labour never starts at all, to the comparatively mild partial inertia when a bitch delivers most of her whelps unaided, even if slowly, and then packs up with one or two still left in her uterus.

In cases of complete primary inertia, especially when the bitch is not heavily pregnant and there may even be doubt as to whether she is in-whelp, the great problem is to know when or if she actually starts. Sometimes a very feeble first stage occurs with a little panting and bed-making but nothing more happens to indicate if puppies are on their way.

A very useful guide is the drop in body temperature which occurs within the twenty-four hours before labour commences. Some people say this is unreliable but *properly* used it is an excellent guide. First of all let us be clear that the temperature of a bitch in the last weeks of pregnancy is lower than average, e.g. $100-100.5°F$, so do not be misled by this. The significant drop is to $97-99°F$ and this drop only lasts a few hours until the temperature comes back up to normal as whelping starts. To make use of this test it is necessary to take the bitch's temperature every twelve hours for several days before she is due; this will usually ensure spotting the drop and one then knows whelping ought to start within twenty-four hours. If it does not it is wise to get advice.

Inert bitches often go beyond full term and whilst many perfectly normal whelpings can and do take place, even as late as the seventieth day, a most careful watch is necessary once the sixty-third day has passed.

Bitches with partial inertia often go into labour with variable results. She may strain very feebly and irregularly and not succeed in producing any whelps at all; she may produce several pups with longish intervals between them and then stop with some pups still unborn. Only experience can enable the owner to recognise when straining is vigorous and meaningful or when it is weaker than it should be and is not resulting in satisfactory progress of pups through the birth canal. A careful, preferably accurately recorded history of the onset, force and regularity of observable abdominal straining will be of the greatest possible assistance to the veterinary surgeon when help has to be sought.

I am always being asked how long one can leave a bitch without getting help. There is no easy, single answer to this. In normal whelpings a puppy is usually born within an hour of the onset of satisfactory straining so, if nothing has happened two hours after straining starts it is wise to report this to your veterinary surgeon, even though it may not be necessary to do anything dramatic at this stage. *Never* allow more than six hours straining with no result without getting advice.

Treatment will vary according to a variety of factors, including the degree of inertia and the estimated size of the litter. Medical methods usually comprise the injection of drugs (known as ecbolics) which stimulate the muscle of the uterus to contract more vigorously, whilst surgery, ie caesarean section, is necessary in severe cases.

I have heard veterinary surgeons criticised for opposing reasons − action, or lack of it! Some people complain that we have or have not waited long enough, some that we have not done something soon enough! One cannot win, and if owners only knew how much anxious thought goes into the decision one makes they would not be so ready to criticise. At one meeting of Scottie breeders, a member of the audience complained that veterinary surgeons rushed in too quickly. On asking for details I was told that his bitch had produced her puppy after forty-eight hours in labour. I then asked if it was all right and was told, 'Oh no, it was born dead!' That is *not* my idea of a satisfactory outcome.

Owners, naturally, want to know what they should do about breeding again from a bitch which has suffered uterine inertia. Once again the advice will be based on a number of factors. If the degree of inertia was slight and the litter was eventually born, even if slowly or even assisted by medical treatment, the advice will probably be to try once more but that, if inertia recurs, the bitch should then be discarded for further breeding.

If the litter was unusually small for the breed, which may have contributed to the inertia, then again it would be quite proper to try again ensuring, as far as possible, maximum conception, e.g. by mating the bitch on several occasions, at least twice at forty-eight-hour intervals.

However, if the degree of inertia was great and caesarean section was resorted to, in my view it is not right to try again. Even though caesarean section is a highly successful operation and, with modern anaesthetic techniques, a goodly proportion of live pups may be obtained, it is nonetheless a major surgical procedure and I believe it to be morally wrong knowingly to put a bitch in whelp when the risk of a further caesarean is high.

It is undeniable that if a bitch suffers once from inertia she is likely to do so again, indeed she may well be worse on the next occasion. Nevertheless, very occasionally a bitch which has been inert proceeds to whelp normally on subsequent occasions, but unfortunately this is the exception rather than the rule.

FOETAL CAUSES OF DYSTOKIA

In this category the fault does not lie with the bitch but is due to some abnormality in size, shape or position of the foetus. In some cases it is arguable whether the foetus is too large or the dam's pelvis too small but this only has significance when one is considering advice about future breeding.

Thus, for birth to proceed normally the foetuses must be of the right size for the breed concerned and must be in the right position to pass through the birth canal.

1) Oversize

This term needs no explanation and from the practical point of view the breeder does not need to know whether the oversize is relative or absolute (these are veterinary definitions), *unless* the diagnosis is that the dam's pelvis is too small for passage of average-sized pups of that breed in which case this should be classed as maternal dystokia.

Oversize is fairly common, usually affecting a few members of the litter; it is uncommon to find a whole litter grossly oversize. It is commonest in breeds which have not been standardised for long and in which there is a diversity of size and type, or in those where smallness is a show-ring virtue when it is customary to use somewhat larger bitches for breeding. This can result in whelps of very varied sizes within a single litter.

If a foetus is too large to pass easily into and through the birth canal it will cause one of three things: excessive effort and increased time to expel the pup; complete obstruction to progress; or failure of the presenting foetus even to engage in the pelvic inlet.

Again, the signs the breeder will see are unexpectedly long periods of straining before a pup is born; evidence of a puppy in the birth canal (either visible as a bulge below the anus or felt by an exploring finger) and no progress even after prolonged, vigorous straining; or, if the puppy does not engage in the pelvis, straining may not be as forceful as expected. Precise diagnosis must be the province of the veterinary surgeon and upon this will depend the type of treatment.

If it is thought that only one or two pups are oversize, assistance with fingers or forceps often results in delivery by the normal route. However, if this is not easily achieved caesarean section will probably be recommended. If the head or hindquarters are not even engaging in the pelvis, caesarean section is usually advised.

My own preference is for delivery by the natural route, ie per vaginam, unless this is going to cause too much distress to the bitch or risk damaging the pups. Although caesarean section is such a successful operation I do not believe that it should be resorted to without careful consideration and certainly not as a convenience measure for the sake of speed! The maternal behaviour of a bitch is at its best and most fully developed when her family has arrived by the natural route.

It is difficult to pontificate on which parent is most responsible for foetal size but I would suggest that if a bitch has a litter with several too-large whelps it would be wise to mate her to a different dog next time − this is especially true in small breeds. If she again produces oversize pups, then call it a day.

2) Head shape

As stated previously, the shape of foetal heads is quite remarkably similar in most breeds. I defy anyone to identify the breed of newly born pups from the shape of their heads alone, with the exception of the few really brachycephalic (short-headed) varieties.

The blunt conical shape of the average head is well designed to fit into the pelvic inlet; the bullet heads of Pekingese, Boston Terriers etc. are not. This often results in a longer-than-average transition from first to second stage labour. Abdominal straining is seen and may be fairly vigorous and regular, but it does not quickly progress to the really meaningful, tail-raised maximum efforts seen just before a pup is born. Sometimes two or three hours of this transition stage may be seen before the real expulsive efforts get going.

It is seldom necessary to interfere early in these breeds but a most careful watch must be kept and failure to progress should be reported.

3) Abnormal shape

Under this heading I am not including the head shape of short-faced breeds which I have discussed previously, rather I am referring to foetal monstrosities which arise very occasionally.

Hydrocephalus (water on the brain) causes the head of an affected foetus to become extremely large so that normal birth is rarely possible, whether the pup is coming forwards or backwards. It occurs mainly in breeds with large, domed skulls; examples are Pekinese, Chihuahua and American Cocker Spaniel. Diagnosis of the condition during whelping is not easy and will be a veterinary matter. It is sometimes possible to deliver the affected whelp with forceps, although it is usually necessary to crush the skull to do this. The alternative is caesarean section and this is often resorted to.

An occasional foetus will develop generalised dropsy (known as anasarca) which makes the puppy both too large and too soggy to be delivered naturally.

Finally, we occasionally see a puppy which has, so to speak, developed inside out with the intestines outside the body, and the whole foetus is deformed. The technical name for this is schistosomus reflexus. Such pups are always in a wrong position for delivery and assistance is essential.

In all these cases the bitch, unless inert, will be straining vigorously but fruitlessly.

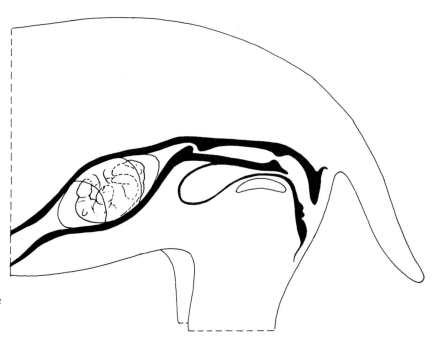

Figure 13 Position of the
foetus in the uterus
before whelping starts

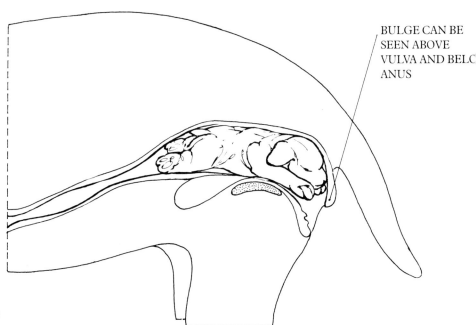

BULGE CAN BE
SEEN ABOVE
VULVA AND BELC
ANUS

Figure 14 Puppy in
normal anterior
presentation for delivery,
filling the birth canal

There is no progress at all and veterinary help must be obtained.

3) *Malpresentations*

This term is usually used to cover any departure from the normal position for delivery (although in veterinary terms we use more precise definitions which it is not necessary for the owner to differentiate).

Whilst in the uterus the foetuses have been lying on their backs partially curled up (see Figure 13). Before birth they must turn over so that their back is uppermost and they must uncurl so that the head is stretched out with the front legs pushed forwards alongside the neck; likewise the hindlegs should be stretched out (see Figure 14).

A very important point in the dog is that it is perfectly normal for a puppy to be born headfirst *or* hindlegs first, ie in anterior or posterior presentation. The posterior presentation is *not*, repeat *not*, a breech. It is estimated that up to forty per cent of puppies are born in posterior presentation. There is some slight advantage in the headfirst birth, this is because the hard, bony head engaging in the pelvic inlet stimulates more vigorous straining and dilates the birth canal better than does the softer hind end of a puppy; these factors are of most importance in the first puppy of a litter.

Occasionally in a posterior delivery the hindlegs and tail of the pup will appear but there is a delay in the rest of the whelp arriving; this is because the head is getting a bit held up in the pelvis. In such cases the owner should give some help if there is no progress within ten to fifteen minutes of the hindlegs appearing. Because the pup is liable to die if it is trapped in the pelvis for long there is not always time to wait for

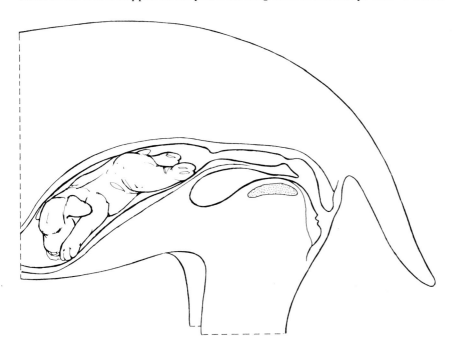

Figure 15 Puppy in posterior presentation, also normal, just entering the birth canal

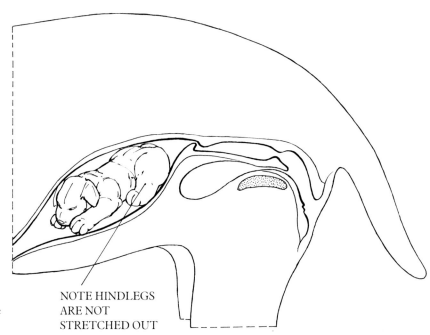

Figure 16 Breech
presentation. This is
abnormal and will cause
trouble

NOTE HINDLEGS
ARE NOT
STRETCHED OUT

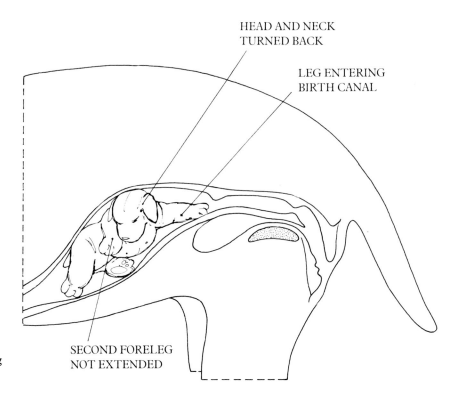

HEAD AND NECK
TURNED BACK

LEG ENTERING
BIRTH CANAL

Figure 17 Wrong
presentation, one
forelimb only entering
the birth canal

SECOND FORELEG
NOT EXTENDED

veterinary assistance. The hands should be thoroughly scrubbed and then, taking hold of the pup's hindlegs as far forward as possible and gently pushing back the lips of the vulva to expose them further, pull gently but firmly in a slightly downward direction each time the bitch strains. If the limbs of the foetus are too slippery to get a good hold they may be grasped in a small *absolutely clean* towel to help get a reasonable grip. If this careful, gentle traction does not result in delivery, veterinary assistance must be sought although the pup may be dead before help arrives.

Various types of malpresentation occur which are related to the limbs and/or the head. Common examples are: breast/head posture, where the chin remains tucked in so that the mouth and muzzle of the pup are not entering the pelvis normally; the head can become deviated sideways as it is attempting to engage in the pelvis; one or both forelimbs may remain back alongside the foetus's shoulders which increases body diameter at this point and so causes obstruction. A *breech presentation* (Figure 16) is one in which the pup is coming hind end first but the hindlegs instead of being stretched out are still tucked forwards along the abdomen; this makes the hindquarters very wide and so creates difficulties. Diagnosis of a breech is based on the fact that the pup's tail only can be felt, no feet or legs.

More rarely, a foetus will not rotate before birth and tries to arrive upside down, ie belly upwards. Or, as a pup approaches the birth canal, its head does not continue backwards but deviates sideways into the other horn of the uterus so that it is the shoulder which is trying to come down the vagina – an impossibility (see Figure 17).

These are but a few of the ways things can go wrong position-wise. In all cases if, despite vigorous straining, no progress is made veterinary help should be sought. These also are cases of obstructive dystokia and the times suggested earlier still apply, ie begin to worry and possibly report after one hour's vigorous regular straining, certainly seek advice at two hours and in no circumstances ever leave a bitch straining longer than six hours without getting help.

If by any chance your veterinary surgeon has left you with any pituitrin to administer yourself on a previous occasion *never* give it without veterinary instruction as, if you give it in a case of obstructive dystokia, not only will you cause the bitch considerable distress but the uterus could even rupture with the risk of a fatal outcome.

In many of the simpler types of malpresentation manipulative treatment will be successful. By the use of fingers and/or forceps it is often possible to correct the head or limb deviation so that the pup can progress through the birth canal normally, sometimes the bitch can expel it unaided if she has not become too tired and sometimes traction by fingers or forceps speeds matters up.

Finally, extremely rare complications of whelping are the occurrence of lactation tetany (calcium deficiency) prior to or during whelping and the existence of a bacterial infection which only shows clinical signs when parturition starts. In both cases expert diagnosis is essential.

Problems Arising in the Few Days after Whelping

1) Retention of the afterbirth
Whenever possible the number of afterbirths passed during whelping should be

checked and correlated with the number of whelps. This is not always easy when the bitch grabs them and eats them before you can turn round, especially as more than one set may arrive together.

If foetal membranes are retained they will usually cause some infection in the uterus, ie metritis. Symptoms shown may include loss of appetite, increased thirst (for water, not milk), dullness, loss of interest in the pups and even refusal to feed them and the development of a dark brownish or blackish vaginal discharge, usually foul-smelling. Temperature may also be raised, but remember that it is often around 102.5°F for a day or two after whelping anyway. Medical treatment will usually result in the retained afterbirth(s) being expelled and antibiotics will deal with the infection.

Metritis can occasionally arise even if no afterbirths are retained. Antibiotics have made life much simpler in dealing with it.

2) Congestion of the mammary glands
In a few bitches, usually those with the best 'dairies', the bitch may show discomfort and even refuse to allow pups to suckle, especially at the hindmost teats. The whelps are obviously not getting much milk. These glands feel firm and very warm simply because milk is not getting drawn off. Bathing with warm water, massage and kneading of the firm glands and drawing a little milk from the affected nipples will all help. Gently holding the bitch and putting the strongest pups onto the congested teats also help. All should be well in twenty-four to thirty-six hours, given commonsense treatment. If the bitch seems ill and refuses food get advice as she may be developing mastitis.

Caesarean Section
As already indicated, this operation, although a major surgical procedure, is straightforward and the prognosis is good unless there has been undue delay in seeking advice or there are unusual complications.

Most veterinary surgeons prefer the owner to have the bitch and pups home as soon as is feasible after the operation. A bitch which has had a previous litter will know all about puppies and will accept her 'caesarean' whelps as soon as she has recovered sufficiently from the anaesthetic, but in the case of a first-timer care must be taken in introducing the pups to the dam.

Keep the pups in a basket or box with adequate warmth from *below* − *not* an infra-red lamp above − and near the bitch so that she can hear them once she has regained consciousness. Once the bitch can be encouraged to lick the pups the problem is usually solved, but remember that both she and her pups will smell of many of the agents used during the operation. What I do is to smear some of the bitch's own vaginal discharge onto a puppy and then offer it to her. This is an almost infallible way to make her start licking. Give her the litter as soon as she is sufficiently conscious to avoid lying or treading on them. This is usually remarkably soon after her return home and the veterinary surgeon will advise on timing as this will depend in large part on the method of premedication and anaesthesia adopted. It never ceases to

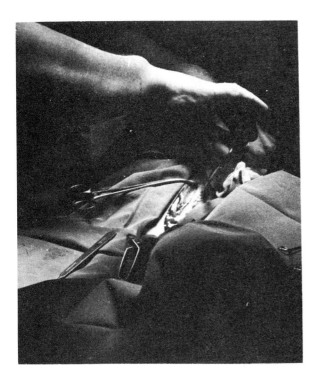

The initial incision is
made

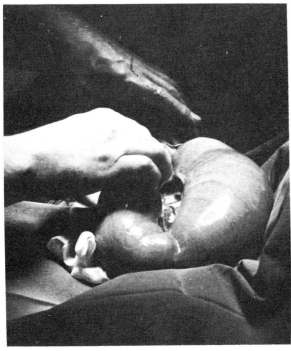

The uterus is pulled
out of the abdominal
cavity . . .

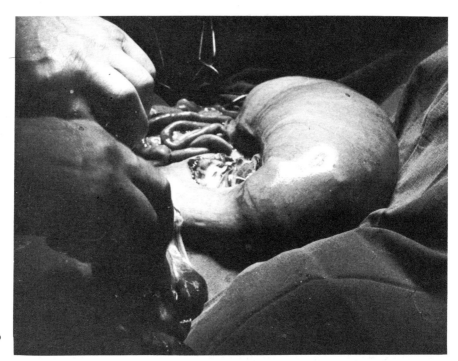

. . . taking care not to disturb the intestines too much

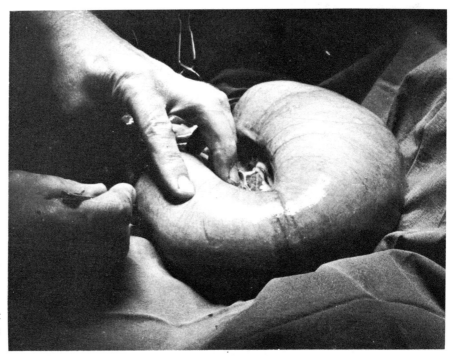

An incision is made at one end of the uterine horn . . .

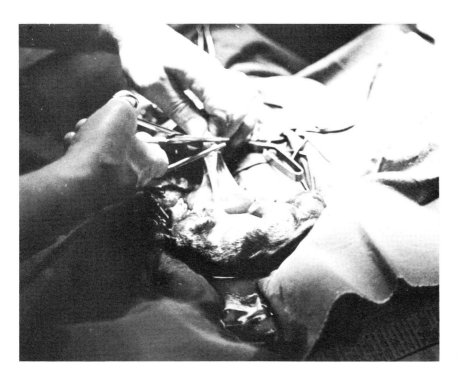

. . . and the puppies extracted and cleaned up one by one.

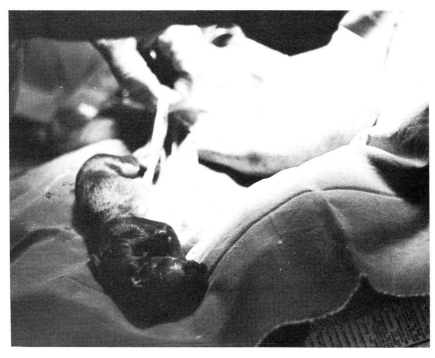

It is actually a much less traumatic birth – for the puppy anyway!

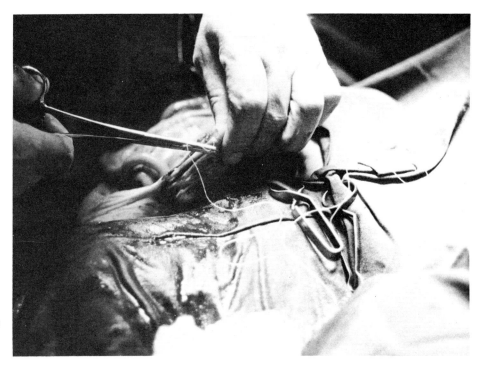

Afterwards everything is stitched back neatly. The vet will remove the stitches in ten days time

amaze me to see a litter of pups crawling all over Mum's abdominal incision and she not turning a hair!

Truly, maternal instinct is wonderful. Let us not impair it by breeding from unsuitable bitches or by creating an unsuitable environment.

Maternal deaths due to complications of whelping are few and far between, although it is not always possible to be sure of getting one hundred per cent live pups. Most fatalities can be ascribed to failure to recognise the need for help and thus delay in getting it. Co-operation between owner and veterinary surgeon is vital and a few points which in my opinion promote such co-operation are:

1   Advise your veterinary surgeon that the bitch has been mated and the anticipated date of whelping.
2   Advise that the bitch is in-whelp as soon as you are sure she is − or ask for pregnancy diagnosis.
3   Report the onset of first-stage labour and from then on report as and when your veterinary surgeon requests.

On most occasions this is all that is needed as the vast majority of whelpings are completed normally, but *if* something does seem not quite right then you are in the best position to obtain prompt assistance.

Nearly all veterinary surgeons appreciate being informed of the completion of whelping. Whether you prefer to have the bitch checked after whelping is a matter for you and your veterinary surgeon to decide. I prefer to leave a bitch undisturbed if everything seems normal, but on the other hand, it can be most reassuring to both parties if a post-partum examination is made so 'You pays your penny and you takes your choice'.

The photographs accompanying this chapter were taken with the kind assistance and permission of P. Ayrton Grime MRCVS at the Veterinary Hospital, Windsor, and show one of the several methods of caesarean section.

9 The First Three Weeks

If everything goes smoothly your new family will do very little during the first three weeks, other than eat and sleep, and this period can be relatively quiet unless there any complications. This applies to the dam as well as the puppies because she will be tired after the physical exertion of producing the whelps and she must now prepare for the chemical exertion of providing milk for them. During these first few weeks, too, she will still be losing a certain amount of fluid and blood. In the days immediately succeeding whelping her discharge will be fairly heavy, dark and rather malodorous. A considerable quantity of matter has to be cleansed from the uterus and this combines with a loss of blood from the areas where the placentas were attached to the uterine wall. The whole process takes three or four weeks and the discharge gradually changes from a rather murky brown to red, becoming lighter as the days pass. This is quite normal and you need only be concerned if there is any sudden change in this pattern.

TEMPERAMENTAL CHANGES

The wide range of temperaments among dogs and the enormous variation in the environments in which they are kept result in an infinitely variable range of attitudes among bitches to their puppies, to their owners and to other animals. My own bitches are all kept in the same house under the same conditions and, although each is moved in plenty of time to their recognised whelping quarters, all behave differently. Some are very protective of their litter while others want to leave them to their own devices after a very few days, just popping back occasionally to give them a quick feed and see if they are all right. All will let me handle the puppies freely, although they show concern while any one of them is out of the nest.

However, I should take no chances and assume that she would rather be left alone and quiet. Certainly, do not allow any other animals near the litter. A great many hormonal changes are taking place within the bitch and she will not always behave as you would expect. Be careful, too, of strangers in your home – strangers to the dogs, that is. Apart from the possibility of infection if your visitors have dogs of their own, there is an understandable tendency to show off the litter. Resist it! It really is not worth the risk. You cannot blame the bitch if she snaps at the person who looms over her and tries to steal a puppy – and do not forget that her protective instincts may even cause her to snap at the puppy.

FEEDING

Your bitch will quickly regain her appetite after the whelping is over but her digestive system has been under considerable strain − not only because her alimentary canal has been squeezed and distorted to allow the puppies to grow but also because she has almost certainly taken on the task of digesting some of the very rich placentas. For these reasons she should kept on a light diet for several days. Egg custards, chicken and fish mixed with brown bread or bran, rather than her usual biscuit, and a constant supply of fresh water are what she needs. After the first few days she can go back onto her pre-natal diet except that she will gradually require much more of everything. Exactly how much more is dependent on the number of puppies that she has to feed, but you will be amazed at the quantities she will be able to consume without putting on a scrap of weight.

I feed my bitches to appetite during the first three or four weeks after the birth of the puppies, ensuring that the balance of each meal is such that it has a very high protein content. Four, or even five times each day is not too often to feed. Her metabolism is working like a supercharged engine and a near-constant supply of nourishment is essential. One warning: do not fall into the trap of thinking that because milk is being supplied at one end it is necessary to feed it in large quantities. Too much milk will lead to very loose motions and will not, in fact, provide the correct dietary balance that your bitch requires. Protein is what is required, plus calcium and phosphorus in the form of bone meal. There is no need to stuff her full of potions, tablets or supplements. If you have a particularly greedy bitch, feeding her as much as she will eat may not be practicable. If she gulps down more than her stomach can hold she may just throw it back up again.

POSSIBLE PROBLEMS

There are important conditions to watch out for during the time your bitch is feeding her puppies. The first and most dangerous is the condition known as *eclampsia*.

I have already stressed that the metabolism of a bitch with puppies is undergoing tremendous strain and one of the ingredients which she is rapidly converting from her own bloodstream into a constituent of her milk is the all-important calcium. If the level of calcium in her blood falls below a certain level she will ignore her pups, become restless, whine, pant and tremble uncontrolably. If you do not get veterinary help very quickly she will go into a coma and die. If you suspect eclampsia you should telephone your vet immediately. Remember that it is not so much lack of calcium that is the problem − it is the bitch's ability to convert it from one form to another which breaks down so any bitch can contract the ailment, however small the litter or however well-fed she is. Your vet should come out and give an intravenous injection. Eclampsia can occur any time between the onset of whelping (rather rare) and the end of lactation and, of course, the puppies will have to be hand-reared for a few days until she is quite recovered.

Occasionally a bitch will show the symptoms of *mastitis*. This is an inflammation of one or more of the mammary glands and may result in the puppies being short of milk, as well as making the bitch reluctant to feed them. An added complication is that milk from the other teats may also be affected. A course of antibiotics solves the problem quite quickly but do be sure, as with any course of antibiotics, that you complete it and use all the tablets prescribed. If you do not it is possible that the symptoms may disappear temporarily but will return later. This second infection will be caused by those bacteria that survived the earlier treatment and they may be much more resistant to antibiotics and, consequently, much more difficult to eradicate. A minor case of mastitis can sometimes be dealt with by holding a hot poultice against the hardened teat and squeezing out some of the milk but, if this does not soften the teat after twenty-four hours or the nipple becomes purplish and inflamed you should see your vet.

The third condition to be on the lookout for is *metritus*. This is an infection of the uterus which may follow whelping if a dead puppy or a placenta has been retained or if bacteria have been introduced into the uterus during delivery. A bitch suffering from this infection will be feverish, thirsty and depressed and show little interest in her puppies, or in her food. The discharge from the vulva will be mucky and dark and have a very unpleasant odour. The bitch may vomit and, occasionally, have diarrhoea. Once again, your vet will give a course of antibiotics and this is usually very effective – but do not waste any time if metritus is suspected, it can be fatal if it becomes chronic.

Very occasionally, particularly with a first litter, a bitch may develop a condition called *agalacia*. This is an initial failure of the milk supply and can usually be corrected by administering a dose of the hormone oxytocin.

Any of these infections may necessitate hand-rearing the puppies, but before we discuss this I do want to emphasise the importance of the ambient temperature in the whelping room. Despite all the horrific and worrying stuff in the last few paragraphs, I have absolutely no doubt whatsoever that more puppies die because they are allowed to get cold than for any other single reason. However good and well insulated your whelping box, I believe it is absolutely essential that the whole room is maintained at a constantly high temperature (in excess of 65°F) for several days after the whelping. Each puppy has a very large surface area in proportion to its weight and will lose heat very quickly if it becomes trapped on the wrong side of the dam or tucked in a corner of the whelping box. I use a convection electric heater with a thermostat which I place well away from the whelping box so that no draughts are set up across the floor. If you remember that orphan puppies need a temperature in the range 75–85°F during the first week you will realise how important this is. Furthermore, it is not just a question of the possibility of hypothermia but one of infection. The temperature of newborn puppies (around the 95°F mark) is much lower than that of an adult dog and a virus infection which would not even show symptoms at normal canine temperatures can be fatal at this level.

THE FADING PUPPY SYNDROME

This is the name given to the apparently inexplicable death during the first few weeks of life of puppies which previously appeared quite healthy. The research that has been carried out so far seems to indicate that it is not one problem but several, and we have already mentioned a number of reasons why puppies may die soon after birth. Others are canine herpes virus, canine viral hepatitis, bortetella infection and some blood incompatibilities (a similar condition to the one which gives rise to jaundice in humans). One case I know involved the over-energetic use of a disinfectant. The owner of the kennels was so anxious to ensure that her whelping boxes and puppy room were infection-free that the puppies were dying from inhaling poisonous fumes.

There is no simple answer to this problem, but you are less likely to suffer from it if you keep your puppies warm and dry and you make absolutely sure that strange dogs and people do not have access to them during those first few weeks. For those who attend dog shows or training classes there is an additional, although marginal, hazard.

Always make sure that you wash your hands thoroughly before handling puppies if you have come into contact with other dogs, and when the pups are older change your shoes as you enter the house so that they do not get a chance to lick or chew them.

HAND REARING

Very occasionally a bitch may die or, for one of the reasons listed above, will not be able to suckle her puppies. You will have to hand rear them if they are to survive and this is not an easy task. You might be lucky enough to have a bitch − or a friend has one −which has a false pregnancy and she could act as a foster mother. You could even ask your vet if he has a client with a bitch which he is treating for this condition. If you can find a foster mother it is by far the best solution because tiny puppies will suffer greatly if they have to go through the night without a feed. If you cannot find one you and your family will have to take it in turns to feed the pups about every three hours or so. At the same time you will have to stimulate each puppy to excrete by rubbing the appropriate areas with your fingers, using a tissue or a rubber glove, of course.

Throughout their first few weeks of life the orphaned puppies must be kept very warm. For the first five days or so they should be kept in a draught-free environment at a temperature of around 80°F. This should be gradually reduced to 70° or so during the following three weeks.

You should have an animal feeding bottle available as part of your breeder's 'kit'. You are bound to need the bottle on a Sunday or in the middle of the night and an eye dropper or similar gadget is just not suitable as it does not allow the pup to suck at its own rate. You should also always have one of the proprietary bitch milk substitutes in the house if you are whelping a bitch. Mix it up absolutely in accordance with the manufacturer's directions and always throw any surplus away and mix up fresh for the next feed. It is a bit of a messy business all round so make sure that you clean up all ends of the puppy after each session, placing it back into the nest, clean and dry, as soon as possible. If it is any consolation, puppies which have been hand reared are nearly always more ready to lap than those kept on their dam so hand feeding does not last as long as it might!

One warning: during the first few feeds the bitch will be imparting colostrum to her puppies which contains, among other things, the antibodies which they need if they are to have any chance of fighting infection when they are very tiny. If the puppies have never fed from their mother it is important that they all receive an early innoculation against distemper as soon as they are strong enough. Your vet will advise you of the most appropriate time.

Hand rearing puppies is not difficult in itself but it is tiring, it is hard work and, of course, you have to take extra care at every stage of their development. One advantage is that the regular and gentle handling the puppies get from a very early age does tend to make them particularly affectionate pets.

GENERAL CARE OF PUPPIES

As for general care, at this early stage it is necessary to keep a regular − but not fussy − eye on the pups. While the dam is out of the way check that their umbilical cords are dropping off and healing properly, see that each pup is passing both urine and faeces and check that when you pick them up they feel warm, dry and full. If a puppy is limp, if you can pick up folds of skin which stay as folds when you let go, or it whimpers and wails constantly there is something wrong. See your vet.

The puppies can neither seen nor hear for the first ten days or so but they can move around quickly enough − and they can speak loudly enough if they get trodden on or pushed off a teat. Apart from this any noise they make should be a contented murmur. If the pattern changes or you are at all worried do not hesitate to seek advice − both puppies and vets have to live!

Unless your breed is one which particularly requires dew-claws to be retained, these should be snipped off when the puppies are two or three days old. Your vet will come and do it for you, but it is very easy to do yourself if you feel that you can manage it although you should ask your vet to show you the technique the first time. You will need a pair of very sharp, slightly curved nail scissors, a small bottle of potassium permanganate and some of those cotton buds used for cleaning the various inaccessible parts of babies. Give the bitch a meal outside to distract her, pour out a teaspoonful of potassium permanganate into an eggcup and, alongside it, have an eggcupful of boiled cool water. The scissors should have been boiled in water for a few minutes beforehand. Take the first pup, hold the first leg firmly and, with the blades of the scissors as close to the leg as possible, snip off the dew-claw. The puppy will hardly feel it − ours squeal because they are being held more than for any other reason and, if they do not mind that part they often do not even notice that anything has happened. Once the dew-claw has come off, dip the cotton bud into the water, collect a little of the potassium permanganate on the end and dab it on the cut. As the potassium permanganate dissolves it will form a seal on the cut and any bleeding will stop almost instantly. You will not necessarily find dew-claws on all four legs but examine each one carefully as they are sometimes no more than a thick, coarse hair and are easy to miss.

This is also the time to dock tails if they need docking. I count myself lucky in that I have a breed which does not require docking, although to be honest I do not really believe that the shock to the puppy's system is as great as some would have us believe. However, if you are not experienced this is a job which should be done by your vet and you should ensure that you know exactly what is required for your breed well in advance. Incidentally, I am not in favour of the 'elastic band' method of docking. If it is going to be done at least let it be clean and quick.

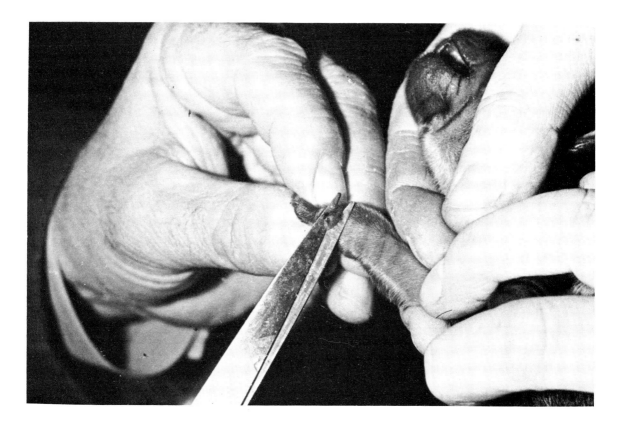

An easier job is cutting the puppies' nails regularly. Your nail scissors are quite enough for the job and it is very simple to do. The puppies' nails will grow surprisingly quickly and they soon become curved talons which can be very painful for the dam as they push at her while suckling.

Removing a dew-claw

I am sorry if all the foregoing sounds as though few puppies have any chance of surviving for more than a couple of days. I assure you that most confinements proceed without any of the troubles and difficulties described here. It may sound as though you will be on the telephone to your veterinary surgery every other minute but our vet, apart from being told that a whelping is imminent, does not usually see the puppies until they are ready for their first innoculation. My experience has been that if you do not know whether to call your vet or not you usually do not need to. Your bitch and her puppies normally make it perfectly obvious if they need help.

10 From Three to Eight Weeks

Things start to get more interesting when the puppies are between three and four weeks old. Their eyes are fully open by this time, their ears have developed so that they can hear and, although they cannot yet walk properly, they can move about at surprising speed. Their teeth are coming through, too, and they will not be so comfortable to feed. As a result, their dam will begin to spend more time away from them and become much more her old self. She will not want to go far, however, and my bitches spend a lot of time just lying protectively in front of their whelping box. As the puppies grow she will be required to produce much greater quantities of milk so she really will be consuming vast amounts of food. Incidentally, her intake to cope with this metabolic level is such that she is unlikely to be able to last overnight without relieving herself. I lay a pad of newspapers down in the whelping room on top of a sheet of polythene and all my bitches seem to know instinctively what it is for. This is a temporary phase and she will soon be back to her usual clean self, as her food intake decreases after weaning.

All the problems discussed in the last chapter may still rear their ugly heads so you cannot afford to relax your vigilance. However, by three weeks after whelping the main danger from virus diseases and hypothermia is a great deal less.

YOUR PUPPY ROOM

Between three and four weeks a change of quarters is advisable, but exactly when you will move them out of the whelping room will depend on a number of circumstances. The breed, the season, the situation of your puppy room and the health of your pups must all be taken into consideration. As with most things to do with managing dogs, commonsense is your best guide.

I keep a thick layer of newspaper underneath the SnugRug in the whelping box and as soon as this shows signs of wetness, I move the whole lot out into the puppy-run. By this time, too, the puppies will want to get away from their sleeping area to urinate and defecate so they will be struggling (and succeeding) in getting out of the whelping box and performing on the floor. If they can get out they will be running about quite confidently by four weeks so they do need a safe, enclosed area where they are not likely to get trapped or trodden on.

The size of your puppy-run will depend on your circumstances and your breed. I have a puppy-run in the 'dogroom' which is attached to the house and which used to be a conservatory before we built proper walls, put in windows and insulated the roof. It provides an ideal sleeping area for our bitches and one end is partitioned off to give an open space about six feet by five feet. The whelping box − with the entrance now at ground level − is put in and this is plenty of room for a litter of medium-sized puppies from three-and-a-half to four weeks of age. They sleep and eat in this area and are put in it when we are out but for the rest of the time they are running freely in the garden. I should perhaps mention that Finnish Spitz do have a tendency to get up and out earlier than most breeds so do not be surprised if your timetable runs a week or ten days later than mine.

You should have been saving up every scrap of newspaper for several weeks now and this is where you are going to find it useful. A layer of several sheets on the floor can make clearing up after the puppies both easy and quick, and you will find a pair of rubber gloves, a disinfectant spray, a squeezy mop and a garden incinerator can do wonders. The run will need to be cleared at least twice a day depending on the age and number of the puppies.

WEANING

I begin to wean the puppies at four weeks, although there is a litter at my feet being introduced to milk and happily lapping at just three weeks! Again, some would say that this is unnecessarily early but both puppies and dam usually indicate when the time has come for a change. If I put down a bowl of milk thickened with an eggyolk and a little Farex (quite a close approximation to a bitch's milk, by the way) they do not have to be told what to do. There is certainly no fixed time for you to start and you should take your cue from the bitch and her puppies. If you have to spend a lot of time tempting them to eat you are almost certainly trying too early. On the other hand, if your bitch is obviously finding the pups a strain there is no reason why you should not put them onto one of the milk substitutes already referred to as early as two to three weeks. You will have to do a lot of persuasion to encourage them to lap at this stage but it is not impossible and can give the dam valuable respite. Whatever the exact time you wean you will find that your bitch 'cleans up' after the puppies much less enthusiastically.

Breeding is hard work, so now that there are several perfectly good complete puppy feeds on the market, which do not require the extensive preparation needed when you had to scrape meat and grind biscuit, I use them − and with considerable success. Follow the manufacturer's instructions carefully and you cannot go wrong. If you want to do it the hard way you should start the puppies on scraped beef, allowing about thirty per cent fat, mixed with brown breadcrumbs or meal. They should receive two such meals each day and for breakfast and supper a milk meal with added eggyolk (not whites) and a little sterilised bone flour, the whole thickened with a little Farex. While they are growing I feed to appetite, making sure that each meal is taken up after about twenty minutes. The puppies' mother usually finishes what is left − the important thing is not to leave it down where it can get fly-blown and stale, or to allow the puppies to get into the habit of eating a little at a time throughout the day. If you feed quite separate meals they will be ready for them and eat well. If they nibble a bit at a time their digestive systems will not work in the way they were designed and the result is almost always diarrhoea and lethargic, mucky puppies. It makes for much more work in the long run.

A warning or two: You should never feed raw egg white to any dog, including puppies. It is almost indigestible and, more important, it combines with an essential vitamin, biotin, which prevents the dog making use of it. In fact, if you want to produce biotin deficiency in a dog you just feed it raw egg whites! Secondly, concentrated vitamin supplements can actually poison your puppies. Because you know that vitamins and minerals are essential there is a tendency to think that more means better. It does not. You can very easily upset the whole of your puppy's digestive system by overfeeding vitamin and mineral supplements, so steer clear of them – and this includes cod liver oil formulations which, although providing vitamin A and the rest, can actually prevent the dog digesting some of the other essential nutrients. Remember that an average-sized adult dog can obtain all the goodness it requires from cod liver oil from *half* a teaspoonful twice a *week*. This will help you realise how little of these formulations is required for growing puppies.

From three-and-a-half weeks old you should always ensure that there is a constant supply of fresh water in the puppies' run. Water is not only a very large part of any animal's makeup, but fluid is an essential and integral part of any metabolic process. This means that puppies need plenty of fresh water.

Finally on food, I should mention that liver is a source of nourishment second to none. Many nutritionists, who you would expect to be very scientific and detached, recommend chopped liver for no other reason than it does dogs, especially those which are weak or sickly, a great deal of good. As with everything else, there is no need to overdo it but a little liver regularly will make up for a lot of dietary errors because it contains so many of the essential ingredients required by every dog.

Having said all that, I still feel that a well-formulated complete food, either tinned, like Pedigree Chum Puppy Food or Boots S-Plan Puppy Food, or dry, like Purina, Dog Diet or Beta, is a sensible and acceptable way of feeding. I should mention that I have tried all the above and that they work. All the big, reputable companies carry out a great deal of research in this field and at one firm's kennels you can see happy, healthy puppies which are the eighth generation to be fed entirely on dried complete feed.

Worms and Other Parasites

About the time you start to wean the puppies they should be given their first worming. This procedure may sound horrific but these days it is perfectly safe and simple. All puppies have worms. There is nothing you can do about this as the larvae are a permanent feature of the bitch's tissue and when she is in-whelp they transfer themselves into the growing lungs of the puppies and start to develop. The larvae can also be transmitted by the mother's milk – either way the puppy cannot escape infestation. There are several common parasitic worms in the dog but the one we are most concerned with at this stage is Toxocara canis or the roundworm. The eggs of the roundworm are only a tenth of a millimetre across but, although small the thick, sticky shell is difficult to destroy and each adult worm will lay thousands of eggs which are present in the excreted faeces of an infected dog or bitch. Eggs ingested by dogs hatch in the intestine and the larvae burrow through the intestine wall and into

The roundworm
Toxocara canis

the bloodstream. The bloodstream carries the larvae round the body until it reaches the lungs, at which stage it is coughed up into the mouth and swallowed once more. When it reaches the intestine this time it develops into the adult worm.

This complete cycle only seems to occur in puppies – presumably because adult dogs are much less likely to have the morbid appetite which actually probes and ingests faeces. As the puppy grows up it will develop a resistance to intestinal infection and the immature larvae settle down in the dog's tissues, mainly in the muscles. In dogs, as apposed to bitches, that is the end of the matter – the larvae remain in the tissues throughout life and few older dogs are infested with roundworm. In bitches the same cycle occurs, until the sixth or ninth week of pregnancy when a proportion of the larvae are activated, re-enter the bloodstream, go across the placenta, through the umbilical cord and up into the lungs of the whelp. After birth they are coughed up, taken into the intestine and develop into mature worms there.

As far as the puppies are concerned there will only be a problem if you neglect to worm them. Although the worms are usually thin there are many thousands and it is not uncommon for a puppy's intestine to be completely blocked by roundworms. It is therefore essential that they are wormed at about three weeks old and then regularly every two weeks until twelve weeks old. An anthelmintic administered in accordance with your vet's instructions will do the trick and the puppies will be no worse for the experience. The real problem comes in that the roving nature of the toxocara larva is such that it will happily drift about and burrow around in any convenient bloodstream. The worms can only mature in dogs but if the eggs are ingested by humans the larvae will do their burrowing trick and settle into your body just as they will in a dog's. In fact, a quite high proportion of us are carrying these things around and it does us no harm at all. Unfortunately, very very occasionally, the larvae can settle in an area that can do some damage. The incidence of this actually happening is only one in several million and even then it is impossible to say whether the damage was done by Toxocara canis or Toxocara cati (the cat version of the worm) or even through infestation from the fox! However, the danger is there. Bearing all this in mind, the complete worming of puppies is obviously most important and it is essential that new owners should realise that hands, especially those of young children, should be thoroughly washed whenever young puppies are handled and that faeces should always be cleared up and burnt as soon as possible, particularly during the first eight or nine months of a puppy's life. The worming preparation provided by your vet will also get rid of hookworm which does not have the publicity afforded our old friend toxocara but which, nevertheless, can be just as nasty for the dog.

External parasites must also be dealt with effectively and immediately. Fleas must be kept off both the bitch and her puppies. You will have to do it the hard way if you see any while the puppies are very young as a spray or powder can so easily be ingested (and some are very powerful poisons). Apart from not being very nice to have about the place, fleas are an intermediate host of another worm, the tapeworm. Also sensitivity to a flea's saliva by the puppies can cause allergy problems later in life. Lice, too, should not be tolerated – they can cause severe anaemia in puppies.

Throughout the period of weaning you should inspect the puppies regularly. They may develop serious genetic faults which will necessitate putting one or more down. Deafness is a not uncommon hereditary problem which I feel warrants this distressing solution, and there are others in a number of specific breeds which should also be dealt with quickly and cleanly. If you are breeding from a bitch of one of these breeds you should know about these difficulties and, if you were not prepared to face them you should not have started! Fortunately, the regular inspection seldom throws up such serious problems. You should check that the puppies are clean, that they have not developed puppy acne (a light rash that should be bathed with Exmarid – a sort of calamine lotion – and which quickly clears up) and that their nails have not got too long. This last is of importance because their paws push against their mother's tummy to stimulate the milk and it can be very painful for her as well as leaving very unsightly scratches on the tender skin around her teats. Just snip them short using a pair of sharp nail scissors while the bitch is out of the way.

SOCIALISATION

Once the puppies have been removed to a puppy-run they should receive plenty of attention from you. They must get used to being handled, whether they are going to be affectionate pets or show dogs. They are developing mentally just as fast as they are growing physically and the experiences they have at this age will have a permanent effect on their characters and temperaments when they are adults. By five weeks they are already old enough to distinguish between what they are allowed to chew and what they are not allowed to chew. You will save yourself and the pup's next owner a great deal of trouble if you give a deep growl when a puppy chews you or anything else you do not want damaged. The puppy will persist, of course, so growl again and give it a good shake. If you get into the habit of doing this automatically and provide an acceptable toy to chew as an alternative you will be surprised how civilised little puppies can be. You are, in fact, using exactly the same techniques as those used by the dam whenever she does not want to be disturbed and you will notice that her puppies do not have to be told more than twice.

By five weeks normal puppies will be into everything if they are given the opportunity. They need plenty to exercise their minds and I tie a piece of knotted cloth to a supple branch of our willow tree so that it hangs about twelve inches off the ground. Running and jumping for the rag gives them hours of exercise and pleasure as do rope rings and cardboard boxes. Apart from the acquisition of a very large, hard football-sized ball, I have never found it necessary to buy dog 'toys'. Like children, they will invent their own games given the minimum of equipment and I believe it is much safer for them to have natural materials to chew or to pull about. I have always been a bit careful about splinters from wood but, so far, I have never had any problems so do not worry about it. However, I seldom allow young puppies to have bones. There is no harm in bones as such but our bitches always get petty and quarrelsome when there are bones about so I just do not get any. If you do give bones to puppies, incidentally, they should be large, raw beef bones – anything else is really too small for safety.

Play is a very important aspect of the development of puppies. During play they receive exercise, they practise skills which seem to be instinctively triggered and they explore social relationships with their fellows, adult dogs and humans. The whole subject of play and the development of the dog is enormous and those interested should consult Michael Fox's *Understanding your Dog* for a thorough and readable study of all aspects of this behaviour. Here it is only important to emphasise that puppies should be given plenty of opportunities to play and, particularly, opportunities to associate with people. Their status throughout their life must be one of subservient companion and the foundations of this role are laid down very early on in their development. A dog will sort out the 'pack leader' in any family within a few hours and one which has been allowed to be dominant as a puppy will be virtually uncontrollable as an adult. It is vital that the owners of your puppies understand this for, although there are many breeds which willingly accept their role from a very early age, there are some which are very intelligent, very stupid or very stubborn and these dogs can make their owners' lives positively miserable.

It is important that, between four and eight weeks, the bitch can get away from her puppies is she so wishes. Even as they are weaned she will still want to feed them occasionally and, at around the six-week mark will probably bring up partially digested food for them. She will see part of her responsibility as teaching them to play purposefully and will naturally be teaching them as she goes along. When you call her, all the puppies will follow so they soon get into the habit of coming when you call even if their mother is not there. As she returns to her normal activities – whether they be digging holes, barking at the postman or curling up on her favourite chair – the puppies will all want to do the same so that, if you have a well-regulated household, you quickly get well-regulated puppies.

EARLY TRAINING

Most dogs are instinctively clean and like to get away from their living quarters to answer the calls of nature. However, if they are only allowed into the house very occasionally it is itself away from their living quarters so you must not be surprised if they treat your lounge carpet with as much respect as they treat your lawn. If the weather is fine I like pups to be able to run in and out of the kitchen as they wish. Even at six weeks they can be taught that this is not the area in which they can urinate or defecate and, after being thrown out roughly a couple of times, they soon get the idea. This ideal situation, where they come into near-constant contact with humans and where they learn to ignore the hoover, the washing machine and the radio, may not be possible in your household but if it is it can be of great help to your puppy owners. It certainly encourages puppies to be bold and extrovert.

Puppies, like children, need plenty of love and affection. If this aspect of their development is neglected a puppy can become withdrawn, aggressive and sexually disruptive. I recently whelped two litters within a week of each other, one litter with four and the other with one. If I had given the matter some thought I should have transferred one of the four to the other bitch but it did not cross my mind until later. The puppies all went into the puppy room at the same time and the differences were remarkable. Both bitches had had previous litters and all the puppies had excellent temperaments. Our loner ate well but he was not interested in the other pups, was hesitant about coming out of the puppy room and very reluctant to play with me compared to the others. I eventually separated him and confined him with the most extrovert of the quartet so that he was forced to take part in the games that were demanded of him. After a few days he had caught up the lost ground and, by six weeks old I had to look closely to see which was the odd one out.

I hope that this emphasises sufficiently the importance of the socialisation period. Naturally, some puppies will be more sociable than others and by four weeks old you should be able to discern differences of character and temperament. The inquisitive one, the independent one, the courageous, the stupid and the thoughtful ones can all be distinguished. Around six weeks old I am already trying to fit puppies to appropriate owners. I have a good idea of the sort of people the potential owners are and I catch myself thinking that the dog with black hairs in his tail will just suit the family with the young boy and the shy bitch will be fine for the couple who have just retired and can finally have their first dog!

With most breeds it is very difficult to tell which are going to be suitable for the show-ring in terms of breed type, but you can pick out the ones which are going to stand up well and show themselves off and this is a good part of the battle.

Do not expect to do much other than watch and look after puppies from between three and eight weeks. They are dreadful time-wasters and, of course, there are few more pleasurable ways of passing the time than watching puppies play.

PUPPY PROBLEMS

As the puppies become more independent and start filling their tummies with all sorts of junk that is totally indigestible you may well find that they develop quite serious diarrhoea. You must deal with this straight away as it can quickly lead to dehydration, a healthy puppy becoming a weakling in just a few days. You should contact your vet if the diarrhoea is accompanied by vomiting or if there is any blood from either end. This could be one of a number of infections and must be dealt with immediately. However, it is more likely that the pup has got a tummyful of sand and the treatment for this is both effective and simple. Take it off its normal meal cycle and do not feed for twelve hours although water should be available all the time, of course. After twelve hours put the pup on a diet of cooked white fish mixed with crumbled brown bread. By the next day his motions should be back to normal and you can go back to the normal diet the day after. This sort of stomach upset usually attacks just one puppy at a time; if they all go down it is almost certainly an infection – go back to the vet straight away.

Another infection that sometimes occurs at this time is one which results from a buildup of bacteria in the puppies' living quarters. If you only breed the occasional litter the bacteria die off, but if the whelping box and accommodation are used several times in succession lymphadenitis, or puppy head disease, can break out. The condition covers the head with nasty boils which need veterinary treatment and careful, patient dressing.

Finally, although the puppies will be bundles of incredible energy they will need a great deal of sleep. From galloping about in an endeavour to take your house and home apart they will suddenly collapse in an exhausted heap. Let them rest and resist the temptation to disturb them every time someone calls who you know would love to see them performing. They need peace and quiet occasionally, just as you do!

The traditional time for puppies to be allowed to leave is eight weeks and I usually let mine go at about this time. In fact, if you have a home that you know is very loving, caring and experienced and you have a puppy who is really strong and healthy, six-and-a-half weeks is not really too early. Some research suggests that it is between six-and-a-half and eight weeks that a puppy will make its closest attachment to humans so, in some ways, it might be better for puppies to go a little before eight weeks if they are tough enough. Tiny puppies and those of the toy breeds might need the care and attention that you can give for a little longer, particularly if they are going to a home with human youngsters. As usual, you must use your common-sense – though it could be argued that anyone who even starts breeding dogs cannot have a great deal of that very valuable commodity!

11 Preparation and Sale of Puppies

If you have described the puppy you have for sale accurately, once you have handed it over and received payment for it your strict legal responsibility ends. Unfortunately, there are many breeders and trading kennels which take this quite literally and do not want to know about the stock they have sold once they have the money in their hot little hands. Whatever the law says, this attitude is morally criminal, if not legally so, and I hope that serious breeders and concerned owners would all recognise their wider responsibilities in these matters. In my first chapter I emphasised the responsibilities you take on whether you are a serious breeder of pedigree dogs or whether your pet crossbred got mismated. Now is the time for those responsibilities to be discharged.

From the time your bitch was mated you should have been giving thought to the homes your puppies would go to. Reputable and serious breeders will have a waiting list for puppies which enables them to pick and choose the owners which they think are most suitable. Building up such a reputation is a long and difficult process but it is the most satisfactory answer if you have the time, the skill and the patience.

BUILDING UP A WAITING LIST

There are particular problems if your breed is not very well-known. Putting an advert for my breed in the local paper would be unlikely to bring any response and the same would apply to many recognised breeds so my own method of building up a waiting list may be of interest to breeders in a similar situation. First of all, I wrote and had printed a simple eight-page leaflet which is reproduced here as an appendix. The idea is to give a prospective purchaser as much of the relevant information as possible. If you read it you will see that it is not designed as a sales leaflet. On the contrary, it tries to be as honest as possible about the breed, pointing out its disadvantages as well as its good points. Finnish Spitz are not the easiest of dogs to keep and there is no point in selling a puppy to someone who is not going to be able to cope with their pet once it reaches maturity. The cost of the leaflet was not great and all my advertising emphasises that I should be pleased to supply further information on receipt of a stamped addressed envelope.

For several years I ran a regular advertisement in Exchange and Mart which simply said 'Find out more about Finnish Spitz' followed by my telephone number. I estimate that I received four or five enquiries each month from this source. I should think that I get six each month from my half-page advertisement in Dog Directory and two or three from my line advert in the Kennel Gazette. The total cost of this advertising at current rates (mid-1980) was about £80 a year (around £1.50 a week). The result is a fairly constant waiting list for puppies from people who have given the matter considerable thought and have gone to time, trouble and expense for the puppy of their choice. My experience has been, too, that having to wait for a puppy does ensure that the purchaser really wants it and, for this reason, I never worry if prospective buyers have obtained a puppy of another breed in the meantime. The system also enables me to pass on enquiries to other breeders if I have a 'build-up' and, in fact, I have recently dropped the Exchange and Mart advert as my breeding programme is strictly limited and it does not seem fair to have a waiting period of more than a few months. This has cut my annual advertising bill by nearly fifty per cent.

If you breed puppies in one of the more popular breeds it will be much easier to find homes for them. On the other hand, the very fact that they are more popular means that your prospective purchasers are likely to be less discriminating and, because puppies are more easily available, they may not have assessed the implications of dog ownership to the same extent. It is your job to ensure that they *do* realise the implications of dog ownership. An advertisement for Yorkshire Terriers in the local paper is likely to lead to a very satisfying number of telephone calls but just because Yorkies are more easily handled than Afghans does not mean that you should be any less careful in the selection of your puppy owners.

If you are selling locally you do have the advantage that you have some idea of the background of prospective owners. Where they live and where they work are reasonable guides to their socio-economic status and this, coupled with an interview, should provide you with the information you need to make up your mind. Personally, I have a shocking memory so I have drafted out a form which I fill in during an interview. It ensures that I ask all the questions as well as reminding me of the answers! I am sorry to make such a fuss about this but if you have taken all this time and trouble to provide a selection of good quality, sound stock for sale then it is only sensible to make sure that the likelihood is minimal of an untrained, gawky, adolescent dog being dumped on your doorstep (or the doorstep of Battersea Dogs Home) in a few months time. You can never be absolutely sure that every home will be suitable, of course, but you should take as much trouble over the question as possible.

PROSPECTIVE OWNER OF A TOVERI PUPPY

Date

Name   Tel.

Address

Contact: Personal recommendation/Dog Directory/Exchange and Mart/Kennel Club/
         Other
Dog or Bitch required
Family
House and garden
Previous experience with dogs
Pet or Show

Other relevant details
Recommendation
Name of puppy supplied   Sire   Dam
Check: Pedigree/Registration documents/Insurance/Health certificate
Purchase price £

SELLING CROSSBRED PUPPIES

If you have a crossbred litter the local paper or local newsagent's display boards are probably your best bet. Crossbred puppies have very little value and they will have already cost you quite a lot of money. You are therefore not going to want to spend very much money on advertising. I should always be concerned about allowing friends or neighbours to have crossbred puppies. Unless you have mated your bitch with particular owners in mind there is a tendency for the family round the corner to say they will take one of the litter simply because they are there and not because they really want a dog. This is just the situation that leads to yet another young dog being left alone all day, or let out to roam or you finally having to try to re-home a difficult and untrained dog.

If you have a crossbred litter it is just as important to find good homes for them as it is for valuable pedigree puppies. In fact, it is more important because a pedigree dog can usually be re-homed fairly easily by one of the rescue societies but the vast majority of strays are mongrels and for the family wanting to provide a home for an adult stray there are plenty to choose from. No rescue society likes to have to destroy dogs but they cannot afford to feed and care for all the nations castoffs and so it must be done. I should think that ninety-five per cent of those destroyed are crossbreds.

OWNERS WITH PROBLEMS

The question of what you should do if an adult dog is returned to you is very difficult. Many breeds run rescue societies which keep a list of prospective owners of adult dogs and most of their work is re-homing pedigree dogs bought from trading kennels which make it clear that they will take no responsibility for the puppy after it has left their premises. I believe that any breeder retains responsibility for his or her puppies throughout their life and I always make it clear that I will be prepared to have the dog back at any time and for whatever reason. In fact, this is a condition of sale!

I have been very lucky, but couples do part or move house or find that they cannot cope with a dog. Under these circumstances I take the dog back and try to resell it. This is seldom easy and, of course, an adult pet dog or bitch is much less valuable than a puppy. However, when I am talking to people about the purchase of a dog I try to indicate on my pro-forma if I think they might be prepared to accept an older animal. If a dog becomes available I telephone these people first and, generally, can find one who will take it on. Failing this, I contact other breeders to see if there is anyone suitable on their books. I then advertise the dog − although it seldom gets to this stage.

I always charge for an adult dog as I do not believe that, these days, people value what they get for nothing, and if it is still young I ask about half the current price of a puppy. This sum is then returned to the original owners, less my expenses which include the cost of telephone calls, advertising and a nominal sum for food and keep. The system has worked well so far but I do recognise that one day I may be placed in the distressing position of having a dog returned which has been so badly trained or looked after that I shall not be able to find a suitable home. Under these circumstances I think it kindest to have the dog humanely put down. Certainly it would be an easier decision to take if it was vicious or ill and I hope I shall never be in the position of having to destroy a healthy dog, however hard it was to handle.

Whenever I sell a puppy it goes with one month's insurance which I pay for. There are several companies specialising in this sort of insurance and, of course, they follow up the cover with an invitation to the owner to continue the policy. If the owner does you are entitled to a commission on their premium. The company I use supplies me with a booklet of proposal forms which I complete. One copy, and the receipt, goes with the puppy's owners, one copy goes with the premium to the insurers and the third is kept in the booklet for my records. The premium is small and I think that it is good public relations to take out such an insurance. I explain to the new owners that I should be unable to replace the puppy but that if anything happened to it during the first month they had it I should feel some responsibility. Infection, particularly, might have been picked up on my premises rather than theirs and I think it only fair that they should be covered if anything should happen. After the first month they are on their own and if they wish to continue the insurance they can or not as they wish. We have never yet had a claim but I still think that it is well worth while.

DOGS WITH PROBLEMS

One thing against which you cannot insure is the emergence of some sort of physical hereditary defect later in the dog's life. I am lucky in that this problem does not arise in my breed but it can and does happen in some and I believe that the breeder must accept responsibility. In this instance I think a full refund should be given and the dog taken back. If the owners are not prepared to let the dog come back then they must take the responsibility and I would not then have thought that the breeder was liable. All this, of course, presupposes that the breeder has not concealed any faults at the time of purchase and, I think, in the case of those breeds which do have genetic defects which may show up later in life, you would legally be expected to explain this possibility to prospective purchasers. Once again, you should not begin to breed dogs unless you have researched your own breed thoroughly and if you decide to take a risk you must accept responsibility for the consequences.

You may find that a prospective purchaser will ask for a Veterinary Certificate of Health. If this is required I think that you should be prepared to arrange it but you must make clear that the costs are to be borne by the purchaser. There is an argument that such a certificate should be provided by the buyer's vet but it is better that it be done by your own as you know him and he knows your dogs. Some veterinary surgeons have strange ideas about pedigree dogs and will condemn them without consideration − they are very much in the minority but it is better not to take any risks. It is preferable for the vet to come to you if a certificate is required because the last thing you want for a young puppy is to have it hanging around at a veterinary surgery.

INNOCULATIONS

All dogs should be innoculated against distemper, leptospirosis, hepatitis and canine parvo virus. However, there is no point in doing this too soon as the antibodies provided by the dam through the puppies' milk will actually inhibit the action of the vaccine. If you are very worried by the thought of infection an early 'masking' innoculation can be given but the effect of this is quite short-lived and the full vaccines will have to be given later. I do not vaccinate my own puppies until they are around ten weeks old and then they have the full treatment. This means that puppies are collected by their new owners before vaccination and I suggest that they take the puppy along to their local vet to get his advice. This gives the new owner the opportunity to see their vet and, of course, he will have a better knowledge of local conditions and can recommend the best course of action. You should emphasise that puppies should not be taken out into public places or be allowed contact with other dogs until at least two weeks after their final innoculations.

SIMPLE TRAINING FOR OWNERS

You will save yourself a lot of telephone calls if you have a simple leaflet printed which explains to new owners what they should do and what they should expect. My leaflet, already referred to, also serves as an introduction to the breed and it is much more elaborate than necessary. A simple duplicated sheet giving feeding instructions, one or two tips on house training, reminders about innoculations, what to do in the case of diarrhoea and what symptoms to look out for which indicate immediate veterinary attention should be included. A photocopied sheet is quite adequate. The important thing is that the owners of the puppy have something to refer to that can answer their first questions. My original leaflet is reproduced here and this proved quite adequate until I wanted to have something which would also publicise the breed.

TASS SHEET
(Toveri After-Sales Service)

When you get home make sure that your new puppy is shown his bed every time he curls up to rest. He will soon learn where he must go to sleep.

Make an appointment to take your puppy to the vet as soon as possible. He will advise you on the necessary innoculations. You should also ask him to supply a worming preparation for use when the puppy is twelve weeks old. (He has already been wormed, of course, but he will need another dose at that age.)

Your puppy should not go out of your garden or meet other dogs until at least two weeks after the last vaccination.

When your puppy makes a mistake in the house pick him up, take him to the scene of the crime, put his nose *near* it, shake him hard while you growl in his ear and then put him outside immediately. You must do this *every* time and you must be very, very firm with him. If you are determined, a puppy can be housetrained within two weeks. First thing in the morning try and get downstairs and take him outside before he has had a chance to really wake up.

You must use the same procedure whatever it is that you do not want him to do. Finnish Spitz are intelligent but stubborn so you have to be very strict with them. You should make sure that you show your anger every time he barks – unless a visitor is arriving or he is asking to go out. Do not leave it until later – it will be *too* late!

Feeding:
Breakfast –	Milk plus an egg yolk (not the white unless it has been cooked), thickened with a little Farex
Dinner –	Meat, tinned or minced, plus an equal volume of puppy meal
Tea –	As dinner
Supper –	As breakfast

Leave the food down for twenty minutes only and serve a fresh meal each time. Water should always be available.

If his motions are loose starve him for twelve hours then feed white fish or chicken mixed with brown bread crumbs for two days. This should clear it up. If it does not see your vet.

If he has diarrhoea with blood in it or vomits with blood in it you should contact your vet *immediately*.

We will always be pleased to hear of the progress of your puppy. Please do not hesitate to contact us for advice, reassurance or just to chat about how he is getting on.
Dave and Angela Cavill

It is always best to ask new owners to pick their puppy up in the morning because this gives it plenty of time to settle in its new home. When a puppy is being collected I make sure that it has a good run very early, give it a bath and have it fresh, clean, and shining by the time the new owners arrive. I complete all the documents at this stage (apart from the pedigree which is already copied out) and this helps me to remember all the various odd items which are on the information sheet as well as giving the purchasers a chance to ask any questions.

I usually send the owners off with a carrier-bag of whatever food the pup has been having. This ensures that the diet does not change immediately if they are not going to follow your advice, and will help them to select food of suitable quality when they come to buy their own.

It is always sad to see the pups on which you have lavished so much care and attention being driven off but I always console myself with the knowledge that they will be loved and cared for much more effectively than they could be if kept with me.

I like to ask all my puppy owners to telephone during the few days following the puppy's departure. If I do not hear I telephone them myself but I prefer not to give the impression that I am 'checking up' – even though that is exactly what I am doing! It is always pleasant to hear that the pup has settled down well and as it is during the first few days that any minor problems tend to arise, a word at this stage can be both helpful and comforting to the owners who then know that they can contact you if they need your advice.

I have left the question of price until last. I indicated earlier that I do not believe that people value anything they do not have to pay for so I do not think that puppies should be sold cheaply. Breeding a litter also costs a great deal of money and, although you cannot expect to make a profit on all you have bought and all the time you have spent, you should certainly try to recover your outgoings. A good guide is the average price of puppies in your breed; another is the cost of the stud fee – the price of a puppy being twice this amount. If you have someone interested in 'pick of litter' they will expect to pay 10 – 20 per cent more and if you have a puppy which is mismarked you may sell it 10 – 15 per cent less – making sure that the owners realise the reason. Frankly, if your owners quibble about a few pounds you should ask yourself whether they are suitable people to have one of your puppies. They are unlikely to get a discount from their vet – there is no reason why they should get one from you.

If you show dogs successfully and you have used a well-known stud dog and a winning bitch the price of your puppies will, naturally, be higher. If your bitch is crossbred I am afraid that the pups will be worth very little. Unless they are specially bred Jack Russell Terriers or Lurchers you can only ask a nominal sum.

Is it all worth it? Financially it certainly is not, but in other ways breeding dogs has a great many attractions, not least when your walls at Christmas are covered with cards from grateful owners who have found that a dog completes their family and their home.

12 Registration and Documentation

The number of pedigree dogs being bred in the UK has given the ruling body, the Kennel Club, considerable and apparently almost insoluble problems during the last few years. Attempts to improve the situation have not been very successful so far and I estimate that it will be many years before the whole business is finally sorted out. The breeders feel that the Kennel Club ought to get its house in order and the Kennel Club lays considerable blame on the breeders for not completing the required documents properly. I believe that it is six of one and half-a-dozen of the other but the whole procedure is very frustrating and you should be warned that there can be considerable delays in registering stock. From the point of view of the breeder, it is important to ensure that all forms are completed in full and that all the adding up is done correctly. Then, at least, it cannot be your fault!

If you intend to breed seriously you should register an affix with the Kennel Club. This is a surname that you can use on all your puppies and which no one else is allowed to use. The Kennel Club will send you a form for you to register an affix and will also send you the rules governing its application. It can take anything up to a year to complete this formality because the name must be published and checked for you may have chosen one which is the same as or very similar to one which is already registered. You are asked to supply a selection of names and one of these will usually be allocated. There is a fee, of course, and you may choose to pay this annually or, if you prefer and can afford it, you may buy your exclusive right to the affix.

The affix, unlike a proper surname, goes in front of the dog's official name if you are the breeder and after it if you buy a dog which is already registered. Give some thought to the name you choose; if you are successful it will be very important to you. It is difficult to give advice but it is appropriate if it can be associated with you in some way. You are not allowed to use your own surname (and there are other restrictions listed in the regulations) but if your christian name is Pamela and you breed Dalmatians, 'Pamdal' would be an acceptable affix. A friend of mine breeds Norfolk Terriers and Finnish Spitz and has recently registered the affix 'Norfinn'. The most important advice I can give is to keep both affix and name simple and short. Complicated foreign words with lots of hyphens may look impressive but lead to inaccuracies in entry forms, pedigrees and registration forms.

Before you mate your bitch you should obtain a litter registration form from the Kennel Club. You should fill this in with the name and registration number of the bitch to be mated and, immediately after the mating, the name and registration number of the dog. You must obtain the signature of the owner of the sire on the registration form as proof that the mating has taken place. Keep it safe — it will be over two months before you can complete it and the dog's owner will not be too pleased if you have to telephone to ask if another form can be completed because you have lost the original.

On the birth of the puppies you can decide either to register the litter as a whole or to register each puppy with your own affix. You will have to pay a fee to register the whole litter and you are allowed to register just one of the puppies within this fee. When you sell any of the other puppies the new owner can register them with whatever name they wish — even putting on their own affix. If you do not want this to happen you must register each of the puppies with its name and your affix separately. This is much more expensive but necessary if you expect your puppies to be bred from or shown. Of course, you do not have to register all of them if you do not want to. If four of your litter are going to pet homes there is really no point in registering them.

After you have sent the registration form to the Kennel Club you will receive a card containing the name and registration number for each of the puppies you have registered separately and transfer documents for each member of the litter. If the new owner wants to register the puppy you have already registered individually he ensures that you have signed the transfer document and then completes it with his name and address before sending it, and the fee, to the Kennel Club. If the puppies were just litter registered he simply sends the transfer form with his chosen name. All dogs which are going to be shown or whose progeny are to be shown must themselves be placed on the Active register at the KC. It is a complicated procedure but is primarily designed to ensure that a dog that is bought, sold, shown, bred from or exported is actually the one that the owner says it is. If you go through the procedure step-by-step, completing all the forms as you go along, you will find that it is not as difficult as it sounds when reading it at one sitting.

When you are registering your litter you have the option of placing qualifications on the certificates. These are:

Not eligible for shows or field trials
Progeny not eligible for registration
Not eligible for the issue of an export pedigree
Name unchangeable

The first two are usually used if the dog has a fault that makes it unsuitable for showing or breeding, the third if you have strong views about dogs being sent abroad (although it will only prevent it being *shown* in fact) and the last if you want to be sure that no one else can add their affix.

You should also give some thought to your own kennel records if you are going to breed dogs seriously. I use a card index with the names of all puppy owners in alphabetical order together with details of their puppy, its sire and its dam. At the front of the index is a card for each litter, under the name of the bitch, showing the sire used, the date of mating, the date of whelping, the number and sex of the puppies and the surnames of the owners of whom they were sold. There is also a card for each stud dog showing the bitch he has mated plus the date of mating and the number and sex of the puppies. These details do not take long to write out and they can build up into a very useful record over the years. Incidentally, most owners do not call their dog the name that you gave it. I put the pet name in brackets after the official name and owners are always impressed if you appear to be able to remember their dog's pet name as well as its KC registered name.

I hope that remembering the pet names of the puppies you have bred turns out to be your only problem.

Appendix: Leaflet for Puppy Owners

This is the text of a leaflet which we give to new owners when they collect their puppy.

Your Finnish Spitz

A Guide for new owners by David Cavill

This pamphlet is not designed to answer all the questions that you will ever have about your Finnish Spitz, but I hope that it will provide most of the basic information you will need as the proud owner of an eight-week-old puppy. Remember that the breeder of your puppy has spent many months selecting a suitable stud dog, carefully feeding and looking after the bitch, whelping and worrying over the tiny puppies, weaning them and rearing them until they are ready to go to their homes. If that work, affection and investment is not to be wasted, then you must do your part. The Finnish Spitz is a remarkably healthy breed and free from any of the hereditary defects which appear in some other breeds of pedigree dog, nevertheless, your new puppy will need a considerable degree of care and attention if it is to reach healthy maturity and become socially acceptable. Like a new car or a sewing machine it is essential that you read the instruction manual first. Failure to understand the mechanism and carry out the correct servicing may lead to considerable problems!

The Finnish Spitz is one of the small group of hunting Spitz breeds and, as the name implies, was first bred selectively in Finland. The breed is called 'Suomen-pystykorva' which means 'Finnish prick-eared dog'. The Finnish Spitz is placed in the Hound group in the UK but it is really a gundog, combining the specialist attributes of Setter, Pointer and Retriever. However, whereas gundogs in this country are looked upon and trained as silent hunters, the Finnish Spitz is quite the reverse. They even have barking contests in Scandinavia!

The breed was almost extinct in 1890 when Hugo Sundberg and Hugo Roos drew the attention of Finnish sportsmen to the unusual qualities of the breed and from a few dogs collected from the remotest parts of the country the breed now has a registration of almost 2,000 each year.

The breed was introduced into this country by Sir Edward Chichester and he, and a handful of enthusiasts which included Lady Kitty Ritson, Mrs De La Poer Beresford and Lionel Taylor, established the breed here. Between 50 and 80 puppies are bred each year. The litters are usually small and breeders selective so puppies are not easily available. You may have to wait some months for a puppy.

The Finnish Spitz is an excellent working and household dog. They are fearless and independent by nature but very gentle and affectionate with their families. However, whereas many breeds of dog want nothing more than to please their owners, Finnish Spitz have a lot more intelligence and commonsense. After all, why on earth should he please you when, with no effort at all, he can please himself? This independence is combined with an unusual degree of sensitivity and understanding so it is absolutely essential, from the moment you take charge of your puppy, that you realise that, given half an inch he will take several miles. They are so delightful, playful and amusing when they are tiny that it is difficult to believe that behind those limpid, dark eyes a stubborn and positively devious intelligence is developing!

Training should start immediately. Give him praise and perhaps a tit-bit when he has been good and a low growl or a loud and sudden noise when he misbehaves. It is important that any disciplinary action takes place as the mistake or offence occurs. If you are angry when the pup comes running towards you he will think that you are upset because he has come – and next time you will have to catch him! Toilet training should not cause too many problems; the breed is remarkably clean and will soon be asking to go out when necessary. Whenever there is an accident bring the pup's nose close to the mistake, give a low growl and put him roughly outside. Leave him out for a few minutes before he is allowed in again and this should soon have the desired effect.

It is not a good idea to take a puppy out for walks when very young, but it is sensible to get him used to a collar and lead as early as possible. Buy a book on basic training so that your dog will not be one of those which take you for a walk. Finnish Spitz are very intelligent but you are unlikely to attain a high degree of obedience training with your pup without a great deal of patience. However, you must insist that he behaves well during his puppyhood because if he gets into bad habits at this stage they will be very difficult to eradicate later. If you have a puppy that digs (and most do!) confine his digging to one particular area of your garden. Stop senseless or persistent barking straight away. Finnish Spitz have been bred to bark over hundreds of years and the Finns train them only to bark at certain types of game and at certain times. You can too, but you must realise that this is a matter for strict training. Never fall into the trap of thinking a Finnish Spitz will 'grow out of it'. He won't if he is not taught what he may or may not do.

The reason that temperament and training come first and that this is such a long section is to emphasise its importance. For your puppy to have an enjoyable life and for your family to enjoy having a dog your puppy must be well-adjusted and properly trained.

Most dogs, and Finnish Spitz are no exception, like to have a place of their own. It can be a proper kennel, a tea chest or even a cardboard box so long as it is kept in one place and it is draught-free. The only sort of bed which is not really satisfactory is the woven basket. They creak and puppies have a tendency to chew them. Some people like to close their dogs in at night and this certainly helps with their toilet training. A Finnish Spitz will live comfortably inside or outside but if his bed is indoors be sure that it is not too near a boiler or radiator. Most Finnish Spitz puppies settle into their new home without any trouble at all. He may squeak or whimper during the first night away from his family, but you must ignore this. He will curl up and go to sleep quite quickly if not fussed over.

Feed your puppy in a quiet place so that he is not disturbed. Leave his food down for ten minutes or so and if he has not finished or has not eaten just remove the bowl. Only try to tempt him to eat if he is unwell. Finnish Spitz are not greedy dogs and will generally only eat the amount of food that they need. Do not be surprised if your puppy is not very interested in his food for the first few days — he will soon eat when he is hungry. Provide him with a large knuckle bone so that he has something to chew other than his bed or your furniture, although you must take it away from him regularly so that he does not become possessive over it. Make sure that he does not get cooked bones or fish, rabbit or poultry bones. In general, the larger the bone the better. Other than the bone — NO tit-bits. There is nothing finer than a fit Finnish Spitz and nothing worse than a fat one.

Breakfast:
Small bowl of milk thickened with Farex or other cereal. Egg custard or milk pudding is nice for a change. Two or three small biscuits or rusks.
Lunch:
About four ozs meat, scraped or cut into small pieces (not minced) with an equal amount of soaked puppy meal and half-a-teaspoonful of bone meal with two drops of cod liver oil. Cooked meat or good quality tinned dog food are also suitable as is cooked egg or fish.
Tea:
As lunch.
Supper:
As breakfast.

Fresh water should always be available. As the puppy grows the quantities will naturally increase. A good guide for puppies is about 1½ozs food per pound of body weight per day, so by the time he is nearly fully grown he might be eating nearly a pound of meat each day.

At about 3 months leave out the milk at suppertime.

At about 4 months stop supper.

At about 7 months combine lunch and tea and leave out the breakfast milk. Your puppy will still not look mature at seven months but he will have almost finished growing. He should have a good covering of flesh but the skin should be loose. Always have a bowl of fresh water available — dogs drink a surprising amount.

Start grooming your puppy straight away. This is to make sure that he is used to being handled and held from an early age. He will eventually enjoy the time and attention of his regular brushing but, to start with, he will almost certainly struggle and make a fuss. Use a good quality bristle brush and work from the tail towards the head, brushing against the natural direction of the hairs. Use a comb (one with metal teeth spaced wide apart) only on the tail and trousers. You may also need to use the comb during moulting. Take the hair out twice a day during this period. This allows the new coat to grow through and prevents your dog looking as if the stuffing is coming out!

Every few weeks check the claws and clip them if necessary. Do not take off too much at a time as you can cut through the tiny vein if you are not careful. If you clip the claws using a guillotine-type nail clipper little and often this is not likely to happen.

There is almost no need to bath your dog. The coat resists dirt and regular brushing is all that is usually necessary unless your pup insists on bathing in the local slurry ditch. It is quite a good idea to give a bath when all the coat has come out during the moult. Make sure that you use a proper veterinary shampoo − not a human one − and bath very gently. It is particularly important that you rinse the coat thoroughly. A shower attachment is the best because it gets the clean water right down to the skin. Dry thoroughly with a rough towel and make sure that the coat is completely dry before allowing the dog to curl up and sleep or go into the garden to dig. We use a hair dryer very effectively!

During the first few months a puppy will take as much exercise as he requires within his own secure garden. There is no need to 'take him for walks' until about six months old and, in any case, it is important that he does not go out or meet strange dogs until well after his final innoculations. Once he is mature he will take as much exercise as you care to give him but will be content with a lot less if need be. You will need a collar and lead (a rolled leather collar is best for everyday use) because it is likely to be many months before your dog can be trusted out of the garden off the lead! Only use the collar if you are going to take your dog out. Any collar kept on all the time will spoil the ruff.

Your puppy should be vaccinated at about eight weeks old against distemper, hardpad, hepatitis, leptospirosis and canine parvovirus. It is usually better if your own vet does this as it gives him an opportunity to see your puppy and, as the vaccination comes in two parts, he can make sure that the two parts of the injections are compatable. It is important that you keep off the roads and away from other dogs until the second vaccination (given at about twelve weeks) has had time to take effect.

When you collect your puppy from the breeder it will be fit and healthy and, for very little cost, you can ask for a veterinary certificate of health if you wish. However, puppies are inquisitive by nature and they can very easily pick up a fatal infection for which the breeder cannot be blamed. It is sensible to insure your puppy, at least for the first year, in case of accidents. Some breeders will insure the puppy for one month for you, even if they do not they will be pleased to give you the name of a specialist insurance company. Incidentally, as the owner of the dog you are responsible for any accidents that he may cause to a third party. If someone trips over him or he dashes out into the road and causes an accident you may be landed with a very large bill. The best way of insuring against this is to ask your insurance company to add a clause to your home insurance policy.

Do not hesitate to contact the breeder of your puppy if you are worried. They will be as concerned about your dog's good health and happiness as you are.

Glossary

Affix	A name granted to breeders by the Kennel Club for their exclusive use when registering their dogs
Afterbirth	*See* placenta
Alleles	Varient forms of a gene, e.g. B and b
Anal glands	Two glands on either side of the anus in the dog which secrete a thick, foul-smelling liquid. They occasionally get blocked if the dog's motions are continually soft and can cause considerable irritation
Anasarca	Generalised dropsy of a puppy
Autosomes	All chromosomes other than the X and Y chromosomes
Brachycephalic	Having a disproportionately short head
Breeding terms	Leasing out a bitch by the owner to someone else for the purpose of breeding from her. A formal agreement and suggested conditions can be obtained from the Kennel Club
Carrier	Heterozygous for a particular gene
Cervix	The neck of the uterus (womb)
Chromosomes	Thread-like structures along which genes are arranged like beads on a string
Cleft palate	Split or gap in the roof of the mouth allowing food to enter the nasal passages
Colostrum	The milk secreted by the mammary glands over the first few days which acts as a purgative and contains antibodies against bacteria and viruses
Cryptorchidism	When the testicles have not properly descended into the scrotum
Dew-claw	A functionless toe found on the inside of the leg and often removed soon after birth. There are some breeds which consider them an important feature so they must be retained in these cases
Diploid	The species' specific chromosomes number
Dominant	Describes an allele which masks the expression of a recessive allele
Dystokia	Any form of difficult birth
Ecbolic	A drug which will stimulate contractions of uterine muscles

Eclampsia	Milk fever or calcium deficiency of the bloodstream. Urgent treatment needed to avoid coma or death.
Elective caesarean section	When it is fairly certain that a bitch cannot whelp naturally and the decision to operate is made before the bitch actually whelps
Embryo	Very early stage of developing puppy
Entropion	A condition where the edge of the eyelid turns in towards the eyeball causing irritation
Environment	All the non-genetic factors which contribute to the phenotype, e.g. feeding, training, exercise
Episiotomy	The surgical incision of the vulva, usually at the top, to allow the birth of a puppy
Foetal membranes	The tissues which enclose a foetus and contain some fluid
Foetus	The embryo, this name applies until after birth
Gene	A coded instruction for a particular genetic development 'threaded' on a chromosome
Genotype	The genetic constitution of an individual for one or many genes
Haploid	The number of chromosomes in a single male or female reproductive cell
Hare lip	A gap in the upper lip which makes sucking difficult or impossible
Hepatitis	Inflammation of the liver
Heritability	The proportion of the variation in a characteristic which is genetic in origin
Hernia	A gap in the muscles in the abdomen through which the intestines protrude
Heterozygote	An individual with different alleles of a gene
Hip dysplasia (HD)	Malformation of the ball and socket joint of the hip
Homozygote	An individual with identical alleles of a gene
Hydrocephalus	An abnormally large quantity of fluid in certain spaces in the brain
Inbreeding	The mating of individuals which are more closely related than the average relationship within the breed
Inertia, uterine	Lack of proper activity – in this context in the uterine muscles
Inhibition	Voluntarily preventing the progress of birth
Linebreeding	A system with relationships between individual mated pairs with one or more common ancestors in the previous three generations
Malpresentation	A badly positioned whelp which makes normal delivery difficult or impossible
Mastitis	Inflammation of the mammary glands

Metabolism	The physical and chemical processes by which the living body is maintained
Miniaturisation	The process of evolving smaller individuals
Multifactorial	A result of many contributing factors, both genetic and non-genetic
Oestrus	The period during which a bitch will conceive
Outbreeding/outcross	The mating of individuals which are less closely related than the average relationship within the breed
Oxytocin	A hormone which encourages milk production
Pelvimetry	The technique of measuring the dimensions of the pelvis
Phenotype	The external appearance of an individual
Placenta	The 'afterbirth' − the means by which the bitch nourishes the puppies within the womb
Polygenes	Genes which individually have very small effects but which contribute in an additive manner to variations in characteristics
PRA	Progressive Renal Atrophy − a hereditary disease which develops in some breeds between three and five years old and which results in blindness
Pyometra	An infection where the uterus becomes filled with pus. Affects mainly older maiden bitches
Recessive	Describes an allele whose expression is masked by a dominant allele
Registration	The official recording of a dog's name and parentage by the Kennel Club
Sex chromosomes	The X and Y chromosomes. In the female the sex chromosomes comprise a pair of X chromosomes. In the male there is one X and one Y chromosome
Sex-linked	Describes a gene located on the X chromosomes
Speculum	An instrument which can illuminate the interior of some organs of the body
Test mating	A mating designed to ascertain the genotype of an individual
Tie	Describes the period during mating when the dog and bitch are 'locked' together
Toxaemia	Poisons in the bloodstream
Transfer	Recording a change of ownership of a dog at the Kennel Club
Uterus	Womb − the organ in which the foetuses develop
Vagina	Usually used to refer to the whole passage between uterus and vulva
Vulva	The external genital organs of the female

Bibliography

Dogs and How to Breed Them, H. Harmar, Gifford

Dogs — Their Mating, Whelping and Weaning, K. White, K&R Books

Collins Guide to Dog Nutrition, D.R. Collins, Howell

All About Dog Breeding for Quality and Soundness, Jean Gould, Pelham

How to Breed Dogs, L.Whitney, Howell

Dog Care, W. Boorer, Hamlyn

Breeding Better Dogs, K. Onstott, Howell

All About Your Dog's Health, G. West, Pelham

Understanding Your Dog, M. Fox, Blond and Briggs

Practical Dog Breeding and Genetics, E. Frankling, Popular Dogs

Index